STEPHANIE DALE

Stephanie Dale read Theatre and Media Drama, specialising in script writing for stage and radio, at the University of Glamorgan (1993-96), going on to study for an MA in Playwriting at Birmingham University (1997-8). Her stage plays include *Wolfsong* (1999), *Sanctuary* (2000), *Blind Summit* (2002), and most recently *Dealing with Dreams* (2007).

In 2001 she was nominated to be Birmingham's regional writer for Double Acts as part of the BBC Radio 4 writers' initiative. As a result, Stephanie wrote *Written in Mist* (broadcast in 2002), with Ieuan Watkins. She has gone on to write *What Is Missing From Your Life?* (2004), *First Bite of the Air* (2007) and *What Is Missing From Your Life? (The Men)*, directed by Peter Leslie Wild and Sara Conkey (BBC Radio 4 Drama, Birmingham, 2007); and *The Wife* (2005), as part of The Gunpowder Women series for Woman's Hour, directed by Peter Leslie Wild.

In 2001 she co-founded Theatre Works with Ian Billings. They have toured over 700 primary schools, secondary schools and colleges, delivering writing workshops throughout the UK and Europe. Theatre Works has facilitated the creation and production of five school-based community plays.

Stephanie Dale currently teaches Applied Drama at Loughborough University, and Playwriting at Birmingham University.

DAVID EDGAR

David Edgar was born in 1948 into a theatre family. After a period in journalism, he took up writing full time in 1972. In 1989, he founded Britain's first graduate playwriting course at the University of Birmingham, of which he was Director for ten years. He was appointed as Britain's first Professor of Playwriting in 1995.

His original stage plays include *Death Story* (Birmingham Repertory Theatre, 1972); *That Summer* (Hampstead Theatre, London, 1987); *The Shape of the Table* and *Playing with Fire* (both National Theatre, 1990 and 2005 respectively). His original plays for the RSC include *Destiny* (1976), *Maydays* (1983), *Pentecost* (1994) and *The Prisoner's Dilemma* (2001). He wrote the first Dorchester Community Play, *Entertaining Strangers*, in 1985, which was subsequently remounted at the National Theatre in 1987.

His stage adaptations include Albie Sachs' *Jail Diary* (Royal Shakespeare Company, 1978); Mary Barnes and Joe Berke's *Mary Barnes* (Birmingham Rep, then Royal Court, London, 1978-9); a multi award-winning version of Charles Dickens's *Nicholas Nickleby* (Royal Shakespeare Company, London, and New York, 1980-1; subsequently Channel 4); Robert Louis Stevenson's *Dr Jekyll and Mr Hyde* (Royal Shakespeare Company, 1991, and then Birmingham Rep, 1996) and Gitta Sereny's *Albert Speer* (National Theatre, 2000).

David Edgar's television work includes the three-part serial *Vote for Them* (co-written with Neil Grant, BBC2, 1989); the single play *Buying a Landslide* (BBC2, 1992); and *Citizen Locke* (Channel 4, 1994). He wrote the film *Lady Jane* for Paramount (1986). His radio plays for the BBC include *Talking to Mars* (1996), and an adaptation of Eve Brook's novel *The Secret Parts* (2000). Two new radio plays – *Something wrong about the mouth*, and an adaptation of *Playing with Fire* – were broadcast by the BBC on two successive Saturdays in January 2007.

Stephanie Dale

and

David Edgar

A TIME TO KEEP

NICK HERN BOOKS
London
www.nickhernbooks.co.uk

A Nick Hern Book

A Time to Keep first published in Great Britain in 2007 as a paperback original by Nick Hern Books Limited, 14 Larden Road, London W3 7ST

Cover image: detail from the James Gillray cartoon 'Fatigues of the Campaign in Flanders' (1793)
Cover design: Ned Hoste, 2H

Typeset by Nick Hern Books, London
Printed and bound in Great Britain by CPI Cox and Wyman, Reading, Berkshire

A CIP catalogue record for this book is available from the British Library
ISBN 978 1 85459 585 0

Contents

A Time to Keep: the background

by Stephanie Dale and David Edgar

A Time to Keep is the fifth Dorchester Community Play. There
was therefore an active research committee already in place
when we were asked to write it. The previous four plays had
been set in the Victorian era, in pre-Roman and Roman times,
during the Viking invasion and in the seventeenth century, and
so we were fearful that Dorchester might be running out of
history.

The most attractive suggestions were a story and a period. The
period was that of the great Napoleonic invasion scare of 1804
(during which, suitably to one of our themes, the young Jane
Austen holidayed at nearby Lyme Regis), and the story was that
of Mary Channing, the last woman to be publicly burnt in
Dorchester, almost exactly a hundred years earlier. We decided
to conflate the two.

Invasion fever

While poring over the newspapers at the Dorset County
Museum we noted how, refreshingly, early nineteenth-century
editors didn't feel the need to invent news when there wasn't
any. At various points in 1804, the *Dorchester and Sherborne
Journal* told its readers it had literally nothing to report. So, in
February, 'the Foreign News received this week communicates
no fact worthy of notice or observation' and, in December,
'nothing of any public importance has transpired'. However, on
9th March, the *Journal* had been obliged to address the big
story of the year:

> *All independent men seem to think that the crisis this
> Country has arrived at is a most alarming and serious
> one, and that the danger is now very near at hand, so that
> a few weeks will, in all probability, put an end to our
> present state of uncertainty. Four things appear to be
> generally admitted: that a violent and great attempt will
> be made by own inveterate enemy; that the Volunteer
> system is bad but cannot now be materially altered; that
> the present Ministers are not equal to the task they have
> undertaken of ruling in these desperate times; and lastly,*

> *that though in all these respects our situation is a very*
> *serious one, yet the union, loyalty and true patriotism*
> *that pervade the Defenders of the Country will insure us*
> *ultimate success against our enemies.*

The 'inveterate enemy' was of course France and its new
emperor, Napoleon; whose Grand Army (and its flat-bottomed
invasion barges) lay waiting at Boulogne. Although the height of
the invasion fear was reached in the summer of 1804, the threat
of military attack by France had been current ever since the out-
break of the French Revolutionary wars in the 1790s. On 26th
February 1798, the Dorchester Corporation 'unanimously
resolved' that 'the sum of fifty pounds be immediately sub-
scribed and annually continued during the present war', and that
the 'entertainment usually given by the Mayor at Michaelmas be
discontinued'. The corporation's only regret was that the consid-
erable costs of building a new town hall prevented it from 'con-
tributing more largely'.

By the autumn of 1803, the level of danger demanded much
more extensive and urgent measures. On 10th September,
Edward Boswell (Clerk of the General Meeting of the County of
Dorsetshire) issued extensive and specific instructions for
actions to be taken in the event of invasion, including the calling
up of men; the depopulation of the coastal regions (up to 15
miles from the coast, far inland from Dorchester); the erection of
beacons and telegraphs, the transportation of over 18,000 people
incapable of removing themselves by reasons of age, infancy or
infirmity; and the requisitioning of livestock, food and vehicles.

Boswell issued a more general instruction a month later, a call to
arms whose rhetorical flourishes anticipate Winston Churchill's
speeches in 1940 (as Churchill's speeches referred back to
1804). Indeed, the plans to counter a Napoleonic invasion were
consulted in the early years of the Second World War, forming
the basis of the south coast defence 136 years later.

As Boswell wrote:

> *If an Enemy should land upon our Shores, every possible*
> *exertion should be made immediately to deprive him of*
> *the means of subsistence. The Navy will soon cut off his*
> *communication with the Sea; the Army will confine him*
> *on Shore in such a way as to make it impossible for him*

*to draw any supplies from the adjacent country. – In this
situation he will be forced to lay down his Arms, or to
give battle on disadvantageous terms. But if unforeseen
and improbable circumstances should enable him to
make some progress at first, a steady perseverance in the
same system will increase his difficulties at every step:
sooner or later he must inevitably pay the forfeit of his
temerity . . . By such timely precautions, the Confusion
and Panic which constantly result from sudden and unexpected attacks will be avoided, and every Man will be
found at his Post in the employment alloted to him, free
from hurry and alarm, and in perfect confidence.*

This stiff-upper-lip tone was echoed elsewhere in the writings of
the time: in July, the *Dorchester and Sherborne Journal* declared
that 'the general wish is that the Enemy may come, and the
general opinion that when he does come, the question will be
laid to sleep for ever'. However, the real fear of invasion was
expressed in a sermon by Reverend Nathaniel Templeman,
rector of the Dorchester parish of Trinity with St Peter, en route
to its slightly desperate, gung-ho conclusion:

*Methinks I see the King and Queen on their thrones, to
the beggar on the dunghill, down upon their knees
crying, 'Lord preserve us!' Methinks I see them now. We
should all go down upon our knees, and when we rise we
should go and take each a pike out of our church, and
fight Bonaparte.*

The war at home

In addition to fears of the French, there were real concerns about
the loyalty of the English poor, who had suffered considerably
from the shortages of (in particular) corn, while their landowning
employers had benefitted from escalating prices. In February, the
Journal published an unambigious 'Address to the Lower Ranks
of Society, on the particular Circumstances of the Country, and
what is required of them in the present Contest':

*To those among you who have formed any false and idle
hopes of being bettered by a successful invasion of the
French, I must say, look at the face of Switzerland and
Holland. I will not attempt to terrify your imagination
with relating to you the murders, massacres, cruelties and*

enormities of all kinds which we have been told will be
perpetrated by the French. Inquire whether there is any
instance, either in ancient or modern times, of the multi-
tude having ever profited by revolution and tumult? Let
me advise you to prefer being governed by your own
countrymen, whose language, manners and customs are
familiar to you, rather than by a foreign foe, who hates
the British name, and all that can remind him of British
liberty. In the present conflict you are fighting not for the
rich only, but for yourselves.

Among the witnesses of Gallic cruelty were soldiers from the
many German regiments formed to defend the Hanoverian King,
some of which were stationed at Dorchester barracks. Members
of the King's German Heavy Dragoons recounted 'atrocities
committed by the Agents of the Corsican Tyrant' which
exceeded 'everything yet published, and chills the soul with
horror at the recital'. The Hanoverians were welcomed by
Dorchester's citizens (indeed, some took local wives), and when
they left for Weymouth in August it was reported that 'the polite
and engaging affability of the officers, added to the sober
demeanour and orderly conduct of the men, has gained them the
esteem of all ranks and caused their departure to be generally
regretted'.

As in 1940, the anticipated invasion failed to arrive. In May
1804, sightings of an invasion fleet through the fog off Portland
provoked the calling of a muster; when the fog lifted, it revealed
a fishing fleet returning with their catch. A persistent legend
insists that, in November, Napoleon himself landed at Lulworth
Cove, looked round, and muttered, '*C'est impossible*'. So, after
Trafalgar, it proved to be.

The Court at Weymouth

As we started to explore the mood of the times, other enticing
groupings started to emerge. Military defences were particularly
extensive in Dorset because of the presence, throughout the
summer, of George III, his Court, and most of his family. The
King had started holidaying in Weymouth (eight miles from
Dorchester, on the coast) in 1789, and took the view that his
presence made it all the more likely that Napoleon would choose
the Dorset coast as his initial landing-stage ('I cannot deny,' he

wrote in June 1804, 'I am rather hurt there is any objection made to forming so large an army of reserves in Dorset where I think an attack more likely than in Essex, Kent or Sussex.')

Seaside summering had become fashionable because of the perceived medical benefits of sea-bathing. (The Dorset coast was deemed so healthy that 'a Physician could never live or die there'.) As the Honourable John Byng reported in the early 1780s, Weymouth had as a consequence become (somewhat unaccountably, in his opinion)

> *the resort of the giddy and the gay; where the Irish beau,*
> *the gouty peer, and the genteel shopkeeper, blend in folly*
> *and fine breeding. At these places there is ever an abun-*
> *dance of the fair-sex, being so well adapted for the*
> *elderly ladies to get cards and company, and for the*
> *misses to procure flattery, lovers and sometimes hus-*
> *bands.*

For Byng, however, the daily routine was far from bacchanalian:

> *I rise at six o'clock, buy fish, read newspapers, walk the*
> *beach, visit my horse; at nine o'clock return to breakfast;*
> *ride at ten, dine at four; in the evening walk beach again*
> *till the rooms begin, cards till ten o'clock; light supper,*
> *bed.*

As Alan Chedzoy reveals in his book, *Seaside Sovereign*, Weymouth entertainments did not become markedly more riotous with the arrival of the King. Life for the now largely adult royal princesses seemed particularly dour:

> *Sometimes they might be taken out in a carriage to visit a*
> *country estate, always taking their sandwiches with them,*
> *or for a sail in the bay. Returning for an early dinner,*
> *they would be required to play interminable card games*
> *with their parents. On two nights a week they would visit*
> *the rooms, and bow to selected guests, and on other*
> *nights would go to the theatre to see the same actors, and*
> *the same pieces acted over and over.*

In addition, they were required to join the King in watching sham fights and troop inspections throughout the county (often at Maiden Castle, the ancient earthworks outside Dorchester), after which they would be entertained by the local gentry. For the

populace (including the gentry), royal visitations were clearly a
thrill. Dorchester diarist Mary Frampton writes of an unexpected
and seemingly informal Royal visit, and the rustling up of a cold
collation of 'partridge, cold meat, fruits, mutton chops and tea on
the side'. ('The females present took a tour of the bedrooms.
They were all good humoured and easy. My garden is full of
people to view the Royal Family.') Similarly, in 1798, Andrew
Abbo clearly found the Royal presence the highspot of his
holiday:

> *September 21st: took lodgings, walked on the Esplanade
> where we met the Royal Family for the first time. Sep-
> tember 27th: wet morning, went to library. Duke of York
> arrived. Walked as usual in the evening. October 3rd: in
> consequence of the glorious victory by Admiral Nelson a
> feu de joie was fired on the Esplanade. Royal family went
> on board Fiorenzo after which we rode to Portland where
> we spent a most charming day. Illuminations in the
> evening. October 4th: left Weymouth for Dorchester
> where after staying an hour took chaise for Blandford.*

The 'glorious victory' was the Nelson's defeat of the French
navy in the Battle of the Nile. Alan Chedzoy describes the Weymouth celebrations from the royal family's point of view:

> *By six o'clock, the King, Queen and Princesses were
> dressed for the theatre. The excitement in the house was
> tremendous, and, at the fall of the curtain, Mrs Fisher
> stepped forward to read a eulogy on Nelson and his
> victory, which was greeted with rapturous applause and
> repeated renditions of 'God Save the King'. Then, Mr
> Hughes the manager, displayed a 'beautiful
> transparancy' depicting Britannia treading anarchy and
> rebellion beneath her feet.*

Free-traders

As the research period progressed we were deluged with letters,
articles and maps from the research group. We became fasci-
nated with the area's thriving smuggling community. As Dennis
Birtchnell points out in his study of Georgian smugglers in the
Wessex Journal (June 1997), the prevailing opinion of smuggling was by no means hostile:

Most people did not believe smuggling was wrong. It was
considered the only answer to the unjust laws which the
government imposed on their 'luxuries' – brandy, gin, tea
and tobacco. The only victim was the distant government.
Payment of taxes, then as now, was not popular . . .

The notion that smugglers were essentially independent traders
standing up for the rights of freeborn Englishmen against an
overweening state was used by many respectable citizens as an
excuse for consuming contraband (as Rudyard Kipling puts it in
his poem, 'brandy for the parson, baccy for the clerk'). An 1804
report from the Custom House at Weymouth indicates the extent
of both the supply and demand side of the market:

The articles generally smuggled from this part of the
coast are chiefly brandy, rum and Geneva [gin]. Also a
small quantity of wine, tobacco and salt, the whole from
the islands of Guernsey and Alderney, which are
imported in casks containing from four to six gallons
each in vessels from ten to thirty tons burthen in the
winter. In the summer season in boats from three to eight
or nine tons carrying three hundred and fifty casks, which
are generally sunk on rafts till a convenient opportunity
offers for taking them up, which they put into boats and
distribute them along the coast at Portland and on the
beach called Chiswell [now Chesil] Beach as far west as
Burton Hive [now Burton Bradstock]. It then gets into the
hands of women and others, who disperse it in small
quantities in the country for five or six miles round.

However, and despite the increasing shortages resulting from the
Napoleonic blockade (making continental products from wine
and brandy to dolls and playing cards virtually unobtainable), we
learnt that the invasion threat brought about a seachange in
popular opinion. Awareness that their black-market activities
were undermining the war effort, combined with suspicions of
disloyalty to make the smuggling gangs seem more like fifth-
columnists than free-traders. As Napoleon himself put it, in exile
on Elba:

During the war with you, all intelligence I received from
England came through smugglers. They are terrible people
and have courage and ability to do anything for money.

Cautionary tale

Just under a hundred years before the invasion summer, a gruesome scene was enacted in Maumbury Rings, an ancient earthwork just outside Dorchester, earlier used by the Romans as an amphitheatre and by their British descendants as a place of execution.

The life and early death of Mary Channing is most comprehensively described in a pamphlet titled 'Serious Admonitions to Youth, in a short account of the Life, Trial, Condemnation and Execution of Mrs Mary Channing, who for poisoning her Husband was burnt at Dorchester on Thursday March 21st 1706, with practical Reflections'. Thomas Hardy mentioned the case in *The Mayor of Casterbridge*, wrote about it in *The Times*, and frequently mentioned its more grisly aspects in conversation, to his wife's alarm. As his 1978 biographer Robert Gittings put it:

> *Hardy in company could sometimes be a liability and anxiety for Florence. With extreme age, his mind and his tongue reverted to some of the less seemly obsessional topics of his youth. One was the hanging and public execution of women. In 1919 with Lady Ilchester and daughter, he recounted the terrible details, told to him by an ancestor, of the burning of Mary Channing, the murderess – 'I tried in vain to stop him, for the daughter turned quite white'.*

In his *Times* article (9th October 1908), Hardy described the case and its brutal ending. As he explained it, the nineteen-year-old Mary was

> *the wife of a grocer in the town, a handsome young woman 'of good natural parts', and educated 'to a proficiency suitable enough to one of her sex, to which likewise was added dancing'. She was tried and condemned for poisoning her husband, a Mr Thomas Channing, to whom she had been married against her wish by the compulsion of her parents.*

Hardy went on to describe the execution itself:

> *There is nothing to show that she was dead before the burning began, and an ancestor of the present writer, who witnessed the scene, has handed down the information*

> *that 'her heart leapt out' during the burning, and other*
> *curious details that cannot be printed here. Was ever man*
> *'slaughtered by his fellow men' during the Roman or bar-*
> *barian use of this place of games or of sacrifice in circum-*
> *stances of greater atrocity?*

Ever susceptible to feisty young women, even long-since dead
ones, Hardy persuaded himself of the complete innocence of this
'thoughtless, pleasure-loving creature'. The evidence makes it
hard to agree with him. But she did conduct her own defence,
and was praised by the judge for her advocacy. And, as the pamphleteer put it:

> *when fixed to the stake, she justified her innocence to the*
> *very last, and left the world with a courage seldom found*
> *in her sex.*

Knowing the geography

The way we connected Mary Channing's story

with the invasion scare 98 years after her death is by way of a
play-within-a-play. There is no evidence that the women of
Dorchester mounted an entertainment about the town's history to
occupy the troops and sustain morale, nor that George III came
to see it. However, the King was an avid theatregoer, there were
many social and cultural events mounted by the Dorchester
gentry to divert the officers, and there was a theatre in the town.
Its manager was Henry Lee, who, in 1830, wrote a book engag-
ingly titled *Memoirs of a Manager; or, Life's Stage with New
Scenes*. In his book, Lee comes up with a striking image to
justify his craft:

> *Whoever is a total stranger to the drama and at the same*
> *time is obliged to have intercourse with the world, let him*
> *be aware of the consequences. He would be in the situa-*
> *tion of a man who sets out on his travels without knowing*
> *a thing about geography. Good plays are as to the*
> *obtaining a knowledge of mankind, what maps and charts*
> *are to the traveller and circumnavigator in arguing a*
> *perfect knowledge of the globe.*

We agree.

Stephanie Dale and David Edgar
October 2007

A note on characters and casting

The Dorchester Community Plays Association insists that
everyone who wants a part in one of its plays gets one. As a
result, the cast size concertinas in and out (usually out) during
the writing and rehearsal process. Our first draft had a cast of
92; our second draft went down to 84. It's a tribute to Dorchester's four previous community plays that we were inundated
with volunteers for this one. Against all our instincts and usual
practices, we found ourselves needing to add rather than to sub-
tract characters from the cast, asking if so-and-so couldn't have
a sister, or a servant (or two servants), or a mother, or a child?
As a result, the character list contains over 115 names.

While all of them are important (almost all are real, historical
people), it's clear that, in any subsequent production, the story
could be told with fewer. In particular, we have increased the
number of smugglers, whist-players and prisoners in the performed draft. Although these groups seldom appear with anyone
else, we have not had to double, except for the parts played by
the Chorus.

As in most plays, not all of the characters are essential to the
telling of the story, and – in this case – many characters could
be doubled and others conflated. We have marked with † the
characters who could not be cut or conflated; as many, particularly those in the smugglers' and prison scenes, could be
doubled, we estimate that the play could be performed by 40
people.

A note on music

The songs in the play – researched, chosen and arranged by Tim
Laycock – are contemporary with the era of the play, or tradi-
tionally were sung during that period. We have indicated the
original song in the text. In some cases, the lyrics have been
extensively rewritten.

A Time to Keep was first performed at The Thomas Hardye School, Dorchester, on 16 November 2007, with the following cast:

ROYALTY– THE FAMILY
KING GEORGE III	Mike Roberts
QUEEN CHARLOTTE	Sue Theobald
PRINCESS AUGUSTA	Emily Taylor
PRINCESS MARY	Tanya Harrison
PRINCESS SOPHIA	Izzie Hall

ROYALTY – THE ENTOURAGE
CAROLINE WALDEGRAVE	Rose Swann
ELIZABETH WALDEGRAVE	Daphne Payne
GENERAL CHARLES FITZROY	
	Anthony Thorpe
GENERAL GARTH	John Ramsden

STICKLANDS – NATHANIEL/MARTHA BRANCH
ROBERT STICKLAND	Vince Jones
JANE STICKLAND	Dee Thorne
MARY SUSANNAH	Lorna Moss
HENRIETTA STICKLAND	Miranda Blazeby
ADA GAPE	Rachel Walker
NATHANIEL STICKLAND	Furse Swann
MARY STICKLAND SNR	Linda Odams
MARY STICKLAND	Natalie Wakelin

STICKLANDS – GEORGE/ELEANOR BRANCH
GEORGE STICKLAND	Paul Wallis
FANNY STICKLAND	Hilary Warren
ELEANOR STICKLAND	Jean Lang
WILLIAM STICKLAND	James Barber

STICKLANDS – PUDDLETOWN BRANCH
JOHN FEAVER	Christopher Pullen
EDITH FEAVER	Billie Brown
LUCY FEAVER	Sarah Warren

TEMPLEMANS
JOHN TEMPLEMAN	John Sutherland-Smith
LUCIA TEMPLEMAN	Lucy Allen

MEECHES
ELIZABETH MEECH	Sonia Morris
MARIA MEECH	Jill Pope
REVEREND GILES MEECH	Philip Browne
CHARLOTTE MEECH	Rowan Seymour
MARY SHIRLEY	Maddy Lyons
MAUD	Thelma Wills

FRAMPTONS
PHYLLIS FRAMPTON	Eileen Dickson
MARY FRAMPTON	Cath Rothman
HARRIET FRAMPTON	Maggie Ansell

DAMERS
EARL OF DORCHESTER	Richard Lawson
BENJAMIN	Laurence Reeve

GENTRY & PROFESSIONAL
WILLIAM BOWER	Nick Heape
CAROLINE HINGE	Joy Parsons
JOHN MANFIELD	Robin Potter
CATHERINE MANFIELD	Tracey Baker
MANFIELDS' COOK	Sue McGarel
MANFIELDS' MAID	Lorna Simpson
MAY SHERIDEN	Di Richards
ROSEMARY CRUNDELL	Vivienne Buttle
LETITIA SOMNER	Beryl Alsop
ANNABELLE SHERIDEN	Mary Parkes

TRADE & ENTERTAINMENT
JENNY HODGE	Sue Wylie
HENRY LEE	David Lucas
OLD LEE	Trevor Williams
ANN HAZARD	Helen Simpson
HENRY BUSH	Robin Mills
A YOUNG WOMAN	Kate McGregor
SUSANNAH CARTER	Cherry Bush
WALTER THE PIG	Darius Whitmore
CONDUCTOR	Tim Laycock
TOWN'S WOMAN	Karen Kurg
WATCHMAN	Jon Oram

LABOURING & RURAL
BILLY LAWRENCE	Alastair Simpson
EDWARD FUDGE	Alex Lyons
TOM CHAFFLEY	Michael Goodchild
JANEY CHAFFLEY	Anne Williams

DORCHESTER PRISON

MRS ANDREWS	Tess Hebditch
PRISON GUARD 1	Darren Richards
PRISON GUARD 2	David Dean
TILDA SIBLEY	Kate Bradley
ROSE SIBLEY 1	Isabel Heape
ROSE SIBLEY 2	Kitty Sansom
MARTHA SIMPKINS	Tina Rutherford
FLOSS	Ann Evans
GERT	Eileen Williamson
IDA	Lee Stroud
MOLLY	Gill Francis
NELL	Elizabeth Irving
SARAH	Juliet Lummes
SUZANNE WORM	Flora Scott
AMY WORM	Kathryn Stratton
TILLY	Hannah Pharoah

MILITARY

CAPTAIN COUNT KIELMANREGGE	
	Joseph Parsons
MAJOR JAMES BRINE	Peter Rothman
CAPTAIN JOSEPH HAGLEY	Lee Fowgies
LIEUTENANT FREDERICK BARON USLAU	
	Ken McGregor
EXCISE MAN 1	Kevin Morris
EXCISE MAN 2	David Reeve
RECRUITING SERGEANTS	Darren Richards
	Kevin Morris

SMUGGLERS

OLD GULLIVER	Colin Clare
PEG	Kay Thorneycroft
ISAAC GULLIVER	Craig Besant
ANN CRAWFORD	Anne Reeve
LIZZIE FRYER	Helen Childs
LOVEY WARNE	Felicity Morgan
HANNAH SILLER	Perwina Whitmore
FRENCH PETER	Mike Morgan
EMMANUEL CHARLES	Rob Sansom
ELIZABETH HARDY	Fran Sansom
CASSANDRA PLOUGHMAN	Valerie Potter
BESSIE CATCHPOLE	Antoinette Woolven
BILLY COOMBES	John MacDonald
KATIE PRESTON	Gean Browning
BOB PRESTON	William Franklin

SAM PRESTON	Jonathan Reeve
TOM PRESTON	Joe Allen
TIM PRESTON	Jack Moss
NIPPER	Adam Childs
POPPET	Maisie Sansom
ANNIE	Lorna Simpson
HERBERT	George Lyons
MEG	Annabel Mayo
EMILY	Sian Franklin

CORPS DU MIME/CHORUS

ANN MASON	Ann Jonathan
BETTY SANGER	Jessica Holloway
EDITH OLDIS	Angie Ramsden
GEORGE CORBIN	Roan Doyle
JANE HARVEY	Clare Daniel
MARTHA AYRES	Sarah Peterkin
REBECCA BRINDLE	Joy Wallis
SARA BLY	Sue McGarel
SUSAN THORNE	Sheila Johns

MUSICIANS

TENOR HORN	Joe Allen
VIOLIN	Lucy Allen
VOICE	Hilary Charlesworth
FLUTE	Elaine Cull
CELLO	Margaret Down
CLARINET	Isabella Harris
CLARINET, ALTO SAXOPHONE	
	Josh Harris
VIOLIN	John Herring
RECORDER	Angela Laycock
MANDOLIN, RECORDER	Alex Lyons
BASSOON, DRUMS	Maddy Lyons
BASS GUITAR	Peter Marshall
CORNET	Norman Mollison
BOWED PSALTERY, TROMBONE, WHISTLE	
	Alastair Simpson
DOUBLE BASS	John Sutherland-Smith
RECORDER	Dee Thorne
VIOLIN, ACCORDION	Jenny Trotman
VIOLIN	Roberta Winmill
CLARINET	Jo Wright

Writers	David Edgar
	Stephanie Dale
Director	Jon Oram
Director's Assistant	Kate McGregor
Play Officer	Sarah Peterkin
Outreach Co-ordinator	Polly Shepherd
Musical Director	Tim Laycock
Designer	Ariane Gastambide
Assistant Designer	Chryssanthy Kofidou
Costume	Rosie Armitage, Maxine White
Lighting Designer	Stephane Cantin
Lighting Technician	Woody Peterkin
Stage Manager	Cath Hylton
Stage Manager's Team	Dave Beeston
	Martin Graham
	Kirsty Riglar
	David Lang
	Rod Drew
	Darren Richards
	Ken McGregor
Signer	Wendy Ebsworth

Researchers
Jill Pope, Shirley Wickham, Joan Kimber, Alan Chedzoy, Beryl
Alsop, Eileen Williamson, Stevie and Colin Durston, Terry
Hearing, Daphne Payne (with thanks to Jo Draper)

Dialect Consultant	Alan Chedzoy

Steering Committee of the
Dorchester Community Plays Association
Richard Lawson, David Lang, Maggie Ansell, Vivienne Buttle,
Rowan Seymour

www.dorchestercommunityplay.org.uk

A TIME TO KEEP

a play for Dorchester

Stephanie Dale and David Edgar

In memory of Frank Alsop

Characters

Many of the characters in *A Time to Keep* share surnames or
first names, and some both. For this reason, some characters are
identified by both of their names. Where surnames or first
names are exclusive to one character (e.g. BRINE, FITZROY,
JENNY or ISAAC), the character is identified by that name
alone. HENRY LEE Snr is identified as OLD LEE, and his son
as HENRY. The older MARY STICKLAND is identified by her
whole name; her daughter is identified as MARY. There is a
narrative CHORUS that performs various roles in the play.

ROYALTY – THE FAMILY
KING GEORGE III † [KING GEORGE] (66), *nervous, liked to
be liked*
QUEEN CHARLOTTE † (53), *contained, cold, heavy German
accent, speaks German to her husband*
PRINCESS AUGUSTA † (35), *coquettish*
PRINCESS MARY † (28), *mannered and gracious*
PRINCESS SOPHIA (27), *flirt, eye for the gentlemen*

ROYALTY – THE ENTOURAGE
GENERAL CHARLES FITZROY † [FITZROY] (30s), *equerry*
GENERAL GARTH [GARTH] (60), *equerry, stunted*
ELIZABETH WALDEGRAVE, *lady-in-waiting, maiden aunt*
CAROLINE WALDEGRAVE, *lady-in-waiting, her sister,
maiden aunt*

STICKLANDS – NATHANIEL/MARTHA BRANCH
ROBERT STICKLAND † [ROBERT] (61), *alderman, bailiff,
bright, no book learning, wheeler-dealer, feels he hasn't had
credit for his achievements*
JANE STICKLAND † [JANE] (50s), *his wife, aspirational,
wants to marry off her daughters*
MARY SUSANNAH STICKLAND † [MARY SUSANNAH]
(30), *third of their six children, sensible, speaks French*

HENRIETTA STICKLAND † [HENRIETTA] (25), *youngest of their six children, spoilt and a bit priggish*
ADA GAPE (late teens), *Henrietta's rather gormless servant*
NATHANIEL STICKLAND † [NATHANIEL] (58), *Robert's younger brother, attorney, Mayor in 1803, smug, doesn't like his elder brother*
MARY STICKLAND † (48), *Nathaniel's wife, mother to Mary Stickland (below), very keen to marry off her wayward daughter*
MARY STICKLAND † [MARY] (20), *Mary and Nathaniel's daughter, impulsive, headstrong, difficult with adults*

GEORGE/ELEANOR BRANCH
WILLIAM STICKLAND † [WILLIAM] (30), *Robert and Nathaniel's brother, not a great success so far, a bit limp*
ELEANOR STICKLAND † [ELEANOR] (60s), *his mother, indulgent to William, delicate, always carrying sweets, everything solved by chocolate*
GEORGE STICKLAND † [GEORGE] (41), *Town Clerk, William's brother, Captain in the Dorset Volunteers, in charge of the Dorchester division*
FANNY STICKLAND [FANNY] (38), *George's wife, glamorous, domestic goddess*

PUDDLETOWN BRANCH
EDITH FEAVER nee Stickland [EDITH] (64), *younger sister to Lucia (see Templemans), a worrier, nervous, timid and tiny*
JOHN FEAVER (60s), *her husband, aspirational, son of a glazier*
LUCY FEAVER [LUCY] (teens), *their daughter*

TEMPLEMANS
JOHN TEMPLEMAN (68), *former Mayor, alderman, Chief Clerk to Magistrates, bookish, pedantic*
LUCIA TEMPLEMAN nee Stickland [LUCIA] (50), *John's wife, pleased to have gone up in the world, hostess and entertainer*

MEECHES
ELIZABETH MEECH † (40s), *high church and state Tory, loves theatre and whist, tall like her sister*

MARIA MEECH[†] [MARIA] (40s), *tall and in many ways similar to her sister, though they disagree on everything*
MAUD, *Elizabeth and Maria's servant*
REVEREND GILES MEECH[†] [GILES] (late 30s), *ambitious actor*
CHARLOTTE MEECH nee Templeman[†] [CHARLOTTE] (39), *his wife, Nathaniel and John Templeman's niece, prodigious mother*

FRAMPTONS
PHYLLIS FRAMPTON [PHYLLIS] (69), *twice-widowed, eager, energetic, lives in Wollaston House in Dorchester with*
MARY FRAMPTON[†] (31), *her daughter, diarist, enthusiast, over-excitable, gushing but nice, elder sister to*
HARRIET FRAMPTON nee Strangway [HARRIET] (27), *gorgeous, statuesque, daughter of Earl of Ilchester*

DAMERS
EARL OF DORCHESTER[†] [EARL] (59), *Lord Lieutenant, Colonel, overall Head of Dorset Volunteers, unmarried, wheelchair, irascible*
BENJAMIN (20s), *the Earl's servant*

OTHERS – GENTRY AND PROFESSIONAL
COLONEL WILLIAM BOWER[†] [BOWER] (60s), *Head of Third Battalion Dorchester Volunteer Infantry, party animal*
CAROLINE HINGE[†] (30s), *his mistress*
JOHN MANFIELD[†] (40s), *attorney, County Clerk, bailiff, Mayor, insecure, trying to keep warring aristocratic factions apart*
CATHERINE MANFIELD[†] [CATHERINE] (late 30s), *his wife, a milliner, flighty*
The Manfields' COOK
The Manfields' MAID (child)
MAY SHERIDAN [MAY] (50s), *visitor to Dorchester*
ANNABELLE SHERIDAN [ANNABELLE] (50s), *her sister, also a visitor*
ROSEMARY CRUNDELL [ROSEMARY] (50s), *doctor's wife, much famed for her honey throat remedy*
LETITIA SOMNER [LETITIA] (60s), *retired teacher*

88

888

88 888

88 888

8 A TIME TO KEEP

OTHERS – TRADE AND ENTERTAINMENT

JENNY HODGE † [JENNY] (30s), *a teacher at the French Boarding School, producer of the play*

ANN HAZARD † (30s), *confectioner, very quiet, small and delicate, different gloves every time we see her*

SUSANNAH CARTER † [SUSANNAH] (40s), *innkeeper of The Antelope*

HENRY LEE Snr † [OLD LEE] (40), *actor manager, florid, scribbler*

HENRY LEE † [HENRY] (20s), *actor and writer, much more into the arts*

HENRY BUSH † (50s), *manufacturer, Billy Lawrence's apprentice master*

A YOUNG WOMAN † (19)

LABOURING AND RURAL

BILLY LAWRENCE † [BILLY] (14), *eager to run away to sea*

EDWARD FUDGE † [EDWARD] (60s), *labourer, father to the Meeches' dismissed servant Tilda*

TOM CHAFFLEY (30s), *labourer*

JANEY CHAFFLEY † [JANEY] (30s), *labourer, and later prisoner*

MILITARY AND GOVERNMENT

LIEUTENANT FREDERICK BARON USLAU † [USLAU], *German Heavy Dragoons*

CAPTAIN COUNT KIELMANREGGE † [KIELMANREGGE], *German Heavy Dragoons*

MAJOR JAMES BRINE † [BRINE], *Royal Dragoons*

CAPTAIN JOSEPH HAGLEY [HAGLEY], *Royal Dragoons*

FIRST EXCISE MAN †

SECOND EXCISE MAN †

THIRD EXCISE MAN

SMUGGLERS

EMMANUEL CHARLES † [EMMANUEL] (23), *smuggler and host of The Crown*

ELIZABETH HARDY † (20s), *smuggler and hostess of The Crown*

OLD GULLIVER † (60), *retired smuggler, wine merchant, distressed by his daughters' respectable marriages*

PEG (very elderly), *his mother*

LIZZIE FRYER [LIZZIE] [†] (35), *Old Gulliver's elder daughter, married to a banker*

ANN CRAWFORD [†] (33), *Gulliver's younger daughter, married to a doctor*

ISAAC GULLIVER [†] [ISAAC] (30), *Gulliver's younger son, charming*

HANNAH SILLER [HANNAH] (50s), *black curls, protecting angel, aspirational*

LOVEY WARNE [†] [LOVEY] (30s), *ingenious, brave and bold, finest female shot in the kingdom*

CASSANDRA PLOUGHMAN [CASSANDRA] (50), *widow, smuggler*

FRENCH PETER (40s), *smuggler*

BESSIE CATCHPOLE [BESSIE] (40s), *widow, east coast, carried on her husband's smuggling trade*

BILLY COOMBS (40s), *smuggler*

KATIE PRESTON [KATIE] (40s), *Billy Coombs' lover, helpmeet to Old Gulliver*

SAM PRESTON [SAM], *Katie's son*

TOM PRESTON [TOM], *Katie's son*

TIM PRESTON [TIM], *Katie's son*

BOB PRESTON [BOB], *Katie's son*

NIPPER PRESTON [NIPPER], *Katie's son*

MEG (child), *smuggler bridesmaid*

EMILY (child), *smuggler bridesmaid*

ANNIE (child), *smuggler bridesmaid*

POPPET (child), *smuggler bridesmaid*

HERBERT (younger child), *smuggler pageboy*

PRISON

MRS ANDREWS [†] (40s), *jailor's wife, and her*

CHILD

MARTHA SIMPKINS [†] [MARTHA] (50s), *prisoner*

PHOEBE CRUST [PHOEBE] (20s), *prisoner*

TILDA SIBLEY [TILDA] (30s), *Edward Fudge's daughter, former Meech servant, now a prisoner*

ROSE SIBLEY [†] [ROSE] (10), *her daughter, prisoner*

TILLY, *trying hard to be a model prisoner*

FLOSS, *bit of a bully, in cahoots with*
NELL, *also a bit of a bully*
JESS, *contemptuous old lag*
ADA, *a jewellery thief*
SARAH, *sarcastic and self-confident*
MOLLY, *jailed for prostitution*
IDA, *also jailed for prostitution*
GERT, *a thieving servant*
SUZANNE WORM [SUZANNE] (child), *timid*
AMY WORM [AMY] (child), *anxious*
FIRST GUARD
SECOND GUARD

CORPS DU MIME/CHORUS
Who, among other parts, play:
ANN MASON, *teacher*
SARAH BLY, *baker*
REBECCA BRINDLE, *milliner*
LIZZIE BENNETT, *hatter*
MARTHA AYRES, *butcher*
JANE HARVEY, *shoemaker*
EDITH OLDIS, *gardener*
SUSAN THORNE, *stationer*
CORBIN (boy), *cheese-seller*

Time and Place

The play is set in Dorset in the summer of 1804.

A forward slash in the text (/) marks the point where the next speaker interrupts.

This text went to press before the end of rehearsals and so may differ slightly from the play as performed.

ACT ONE

Prologue – 'The perfect place in history to be'

Dorchester, 7th September 1804. As the audience enters, they may be pleasantly surprised to find themselves in a theatre, with proscenium and maybe even a curtain. After they are all assembled, two Royal EQUERRIES, GENERAL GARTH *and* GENERAL CHARLES FITZROY *appear, announcing the entrance of the* ROYAL PARTY.

GARTH. His Majesty! His Majesty King George! Her Majesty the Queen!

FITZROY. Make way for Their Royal Highnesses the Princesses Augusta, Mary and Sophia!

FITZROY *and* GARTH. Look sharp! Look sharp!

Everyone bows as the ROYAL PARTY *enters:* KING GEORGE, QUEEN CHARLOTTE, *the* PRINCESSES AUGUSTA, MARY, *and* SOPHIA, *followed by their ladies-in-waiting* ELIZABETH WALDEGRAVE *and* CAROLINE WALDEGRAVE. *They make their way to the Royal Box and sit. Everyone applauds. The* CONDUCTOR *raises his baton to start the music, when* KING GEORGE *raises his finger. The music stops after two notes.* KING GEORGE *then blows his nose. Then he nods to the* CONDUCTOR *who conducts the opening fanfare. The curtain rises, and a* WOMAN *dressed in a rough-and-ready man's costume walks on to the stage. She is* JENNY HODGE, *joined by the* CHORUS.

JENNY.
    Good gentles, and most gentle Majesty:
    A fanfare heralds high solemnity.
    So who is this poor creature to aspire
    To act as prologue, in this mean attire?

CHORUS.
>   First to confess, that for our revelling
>   We'd hoped for nobles, never yet a king.
>   To hear our tale which starts in long lost time,
>   As monuments arose from ancient slime.
>   To our own age of amity and grace,
>   Where sect and faction affably embrace.
>   The fourth year of the nineteenth century:
>   The perfect place in history to be!

JENNY.
>   How may our tale be told without offence?
>   Some doubt our talent, others the expense.
>   While critics question our dramatic mode:

CHORUS.
>   'Why not an opera?', 'Why not an ode?'
>   Despite all this, we nonetheless avow:
>   All arts before the Muse of Thespis bow.
>   So reaching the conclusion that, today
>   Our history is best told through –

Suddenly, the voice of an irascible and gouty old man booms out.

He is the EARL OF DORCHESTER, *in a wheelchair pushed on by a long-suffering servant,* BENJAMIN. *As he speaks, the setting transforms from the play into a public meeting.*

EARL. A play? At this moment of utmost peril, as our island people stands alone against the full might of Napoleon and his Gallic hordes, we are summoned to discuss the presentation of a *play*?

Scene One – 'At this time of national jeopardy'

Towards the end of a public meeting, held two months earlier in Dorchester, on Monday 2nd July. Chaired by the Mayor JOHN MANFIELD, *who sits next to the Town Clerk* GEORGE STICKLAND, *the meeting is predominantly but not entirely male.* ATTENDEES *include the* EARL, COLONEL WILLIAM BOWER, *his friend* CAROLINE HINGE, GEORGE's *mother* ELEANOR STICKLAND *and his younger brother* WILLIAM STICKLAND, *his distant cousins* ROBERT STICKLAND *and* NATHANIEL STICKLAND *with their wives* JANE STICKLAND *and* MARY STICKLAND, HENRY BUSH, *Antelope Innkeeper* SUSANNAH CARTER, *the Misses* ELIZABETH MEECH *and* MARIA MEECH, *former Mayor* JOHN TEMPLEMAN *and his wife* LUCIA TEMPLEMAN, *the theatrical manager* OLD LEE *and his son* HENRY LEE, *and French teacher* JENNY.

JOHN MANFIELD. Well, as I understand it, my lord, this is one of a number of proposals to . . . to . . .

GEORGE (*prompting*). To improve morale, at this time of national jeopardy.

JOHN MANFIELD. Along with all the other measures we have implemented, to protect our town and county from . . .

EARL. . . . . the imminent invasionary threat!

JENNY *steps forward*.

JENNY. Mr Mayor, the proposal's mine.

Pause.

JOHN MANFIELD. Miss, um . . .

JENNY. My name is Jenny Hodge. I am employed at the French Boarding School.

EARL. Aha!

JENNY. My proposal is to encourage the flower of our town to come together to produce a play about its history.

SUSANNAH. Well, that'll drive Boney back into the briny.

JENNY. To involve both the British and Hanoverian Regiments currently barracked in the town–

MARIA. Hanoverians? Our young ladies to consort with Hanoverians?

ELIZABETH MEECH. Sister.

JENNY. – that they may understand us, and we them. That furthermore we bring together persons of all classes . . .

EARL. Hmph!

JENNY. – as participants and auditors, and be reminded of those great principles for which we fight and the grand traditions that make England what it is.

Silence and bemusement.

NATHANIEL. And when you say 'the history'?

JENNY. I mean the great events and lesser incidents which have shaped our town, and the noted and notorious personages for whom it's famed.

ROBERT. And how is all this to be paid for?

JENNY. I am sure that this endeavour will attract an extensive audience.

OLD LEE. Hmphh.

JENNY. On the other hand, it is true that we will have need of somewhere to rehearse, and indeed perform.

OLD LEE. Not in my theatre.

JENNY. And capital for investment in the properties and costumes, particularly at this time of general shortage –

MARIA. 'Investment'!

ELIZABETH MEECH. Please, Maria.

JOHN TEMPLEMAN. Perhaps, Mr Mayor, this matter might be referred to a meeting of the council.

EARL. Sometime in the not too immediate future.

JOHN MANFIELD. Well, certainly, if that meets with general approval . . .

Calls of 'Hear, hear!' from most people.

GEORGE. Passed by acclamation.

JENNY. But Mr Mayor, if we are to mount the play before the harvest –

JOHN MANFIELD. I . . . declare the meeting closed.

The meeting breaks up. BENJAMIN *wheels the* EARL *past* JENNY.

EARL. The French Academy, you say?

JENNY. I spent many of my younger years in France.

EARL. And you come back here to mount a play?

Not waiting for a reply.

Benjamin. Home!

BENJAMIN. Yes, of course, m'lord . . .

The BROTHERS STICKLAND *and their wives walk out on to High West Street.* ROBERT's *daughter* MARY *is walking along.*

ROBERT. Nathaniel.

NATHANIEL. Brother.

ROBERT. Is that not my niece Mary at the corner?

NATHANIEL. Yes.

MARY STICKLAND. Mary!

MARY. Oh, Mama. Papa.

NATHANIEL (*waving his fobwatch, a regular gesture*). Mary, were you not instructed to occupy the hours between five and seven at your new piano?

MARY STICKLAND. In fact, I think, her petit-point.

MARY. Oh, but Mama. I was suffocking. I went out into the fields.

ROBERT. The fields?

NATHANIEL. Home with your mother, Mary.

MARY. Yes, at once, Papa.

For MARY *has seen* GEORGE, *his mother* ELEANOR *and brother* WILLIAM *come out of the meeting.* MARY *takes her mother's arm and nearly pulls her away.*

MARY STICKLAND (*over her shoulder*). Nathaniel!

ROBERT. A new piano, brother?

NATHANIEL. Yes. However . . .

Nodding in WILLIAM's *direction.*

I understand her distant cousin William has set his eye on her.

ROBERT (*going*). Good luck.

NATHANIEL (*to himself*). A play?

Back in the meeting room, the stragglers include JENNY, HENRY *and* ELIZABETH MEECH.

HENRY. Miss Hodge. My name is Henry Lee. My father is proprietor of the North Square Theatre.

JENNY. The one who said 'not in my / theatre . . . '

HENRY. I, on the other hand, would be happy to offer my services. As an advisor to your innovative enterprise.

JENNY. I am . . . quite sure we need advice.

HENRY *smiles and leaves, as* ELIZABETH MEECH *approaches* JENNY.

ELIZABETH MEECH. Miss Hodge. My name is Elizabeth Meech. My sister complained about the Hanoverians.

MARIA. Elizabeth!

ELIZABETH MEECH. We spend many hours with ladies of great influence and reputation in the town.

MARIA. Sister, please!

ELIZABETH MEECH. So, when do we begin?

As JENNY *and* ELIZABETH MEECH *move into the next scene, a servant girl called* ADA GAPE *sings 'If I Was a Blackbird', not very well; whilst the* CHORUS *appears, to explain what is happening.*

ADA GAPE.
    If I was a blackbird, I'd whistle and sing
    I'd follow the ship that my true love sails in
    And on the top rigging there I'd build my nest
    And lay my dark head on his lyly-white breast.

    If I was a scholar, could handle a pen
    Just one private letter to him I would send
    I'd write and I'd tell him of my sorrow and woe
    And straight o'er the ocean to my true love I'd go.

CHORUS. And despite the half-hearted response of the Greatest Figures in the Town

– Miss Hodge produced a Bill informing the gentry and citizenry that all those with a talent for the Thespian Arts

– were invited on the 17th of July 1804 to attend at the upstairs room of The Antelope Hotel

– the hire of which would be affrayed by means as yet unresolved

– for a Grand Audition!

Scene Two – 'Do you have any other talents?'

The audition line-up is JENNY, ELIZABETH MEECH, *and* HENRY. SUSANNAH *is serving drinks to the audition team and then goes out.* ADA GAPE *concludes her disastrous audition song, to everyone's relief.*

JENNY. Next. Next!

HENRY. Thank you.

ADA GAPE *goes and sits on a bench with a small group of other* AUDITIONEES, *crossing with* ANN HAZARD, *a confectioner, who enters from another room.*

ELIZABETH MEECH. Good Afternoon. It's Miss Hazard, is it not?

ANN HAZARD (*virtually inaudible*). Yes.

JENNY. The proprietor of the confectioner's on High West Street?

ANN HAZARD *nods.*

HENRY. Perhaps Miss Hazard might read out the speech we gave her.

ANN HAZARD *has a sheet of paper from which she reads, very quietly.*

ANN HAZARD. 'Mary defiantly Mother do you not remember . . . '

JENNY. Forgive me, Miss Hazard, you don't need to read out 'Mary'. It's the name of the character who says the speech.

ANN HAZARD. Oh.

ELIZABETH MEECH. Nor 'defiantly'.

HENRY. Which is how she says it.

JENNY. So it begins 'Mother, do you not remember . . . ?'

ANN HAZARD. Yes.

Still very quietly, and very fast.

'Mother, do you not remember how you were absent for most of my abandoned childhood. Do you not recall how at my finishing you sent me to the capital.'

She drops the script.

'To the capital . . . '

JENNY. Thank you, Miss Hazard.

ELIZABETH MEECH. If you wish, please join the others.

ANN HAZARD (*inaudibly*). Thank you.

HENRY. And, next?

ELIZABETH MEECH (*reading from the list, calls*). Mrs Manfield.

ANN HAZARD *sits next to* ADA GAPE *as* CATHERINE MANFIELD *enters.* HENRY *gestures to* ANN HAZARD *to give him the audition speech. During the following, half-surrepticiously, he amends it.*

JENNY (*to* HENRY). Mrs Manfield oversees a millinery establishment in South Street.

ELIZABETH MEECH. And is Married To The Mayor.

HENRY. Mrs Manfield, have you read the speech?

CATHERINE. Yes. Can I presume the character who delivers it is a major figure in the play?

JENNY. Of course, we are hearing many people for all parts . . .

CATHERINE. But not everyone is married to the Mayor. Who is of course presently considering whether to support / this venture.

ELIZABETH MEECH. We take your point, Mrs Manfield.

JENNY. Now, perhaps –

CATHERINE (*suddenly, with a great gesture, melodramatically*). 'Mother, do you not remember how you were absent for most of my abandoned childhood? Do you not recall how at my finishing you sent me to the capital? Was it not you who presented me a glittering jewel box

JENNY. Uh . . .

CATHERINE. – and then slammed it

HENRY. Mrs Manfield.

CATHERINE. – shut upon my fingers!' Of course, once rehearsed, I would do it all with considerably more passion.

ELIZABETH MEECH. Thank you.

CATHERINE. Mr Lee, do you have an immediate response to my performance?

All eyes turn in HENRY's *direction*.

HENRY. We have certainly seen nothing quite like it.

CATHERINE. Thank you.

CATHERINE *sits on a chair with* ANN HAZARD *and* ADA GAPE. *Meanwhile* SUSANNAH *admits a group:* WILLIAM *is led into the room by his distant cousins* HENRIETTA STICKLAND *and* MARY SUSANNAH STICKLAND. *There is a twitter of excitement on the judges' table as so many young people are seen entering the room.* ADA GAPE *turns her face away to conceal herself from* HENRIETTA. SUSANNAH *goes out.*

JENNY. Who is next, Miss Meech?

HENRY. An abundance of riches.

HENRIETTA. In fact there is only one of us auditioning.

HENRY. And which may that / be . . . ?

MARY SUSANNAH. Our cousin, William.

ELIZABETH MEECH (*whispers to* JENNY). Brother To The Town Clerk.

HENRIETTA. To improve his confidence and poise.

HENRY. You have brought the piece to read?

WILLIAM. Yes, though I fear . . .

HENRIETTA. And whatever apprehensions he may feel . . .

MARY SUSANNAH. . . . . he will rise above them.

HENRIETTA. Will he not?

JENNY. The speech is taken from a sermon, delivered by John White, a pastor here in Dorchester nearly two hundred years ago.

WILLIAM (*with a look to* HENRIETTA). A p-p-p-pastor. As I said.

HENRY (*recognising the problem*). Ah.

JENNY. In your own time, Mr Stickland.

WILLIAM (*reads*). 'Today is midsummer – the day we celebrate the Nativity of the Blessed John the Bap-ptist. Like the p-p-prophet John p-p-preaching in the wilderness – '

HENRY. Thank you, Mr Stickland.

JENNY. I wonder, apart from acting, do you have any other talents?

MARY SUSANNAH. Miss Meech, does anybody die in your play?

ELIZABETH MEECH. Many people.

HENRIETTA. Well, there you are. William must do his party piece.

WILLIAM. Oh, no . . .

JENNY. What's that?

MARY SUSANNAH. Oh, come on, William. It has everyone in stitches at Christmas.

HENRIETTA. Even your brother . . .

HENRIETTA *and* MARY SUSANNAH. The Town Clerk.

MARY SUSANNAH. And if you're seriously intending to remedy your single status before *next* / Christmas . . .

HENRIETTA (*dramatically but rather well*).
    And so Brave Will took poison
    The headsman for to foil . . .

WILLIAM *accepts the inevitable and does a dramatic and acrobatic death scene as* HENRIETTA *continues, with* MARY SUSANNAH *providing musical accompaniment.*

    And fell upon the cold grey flags
    All in a sort of coil.

Spontaneous round of applause.

MARY SUSANNAH. And there you are.

JENNY. Well, Mr Stickland, I'm sure we'll find a part for you.

HENRIETTA. William, you can get up now. We need you to escort us to High East Street. . .

HENRY. Um, Miss Stickland?

HENRIETTA. Yes?

HENRY. I wonder, could you read that out? From there?

JENNY. She's speaking to her mother.

She hands HENRIETTA *a script. She reads it, quickly, efficiently and effectively.*

HENRIETTA. I see. 'Was it not you who presented me a glittering jewel box and then slammed it shut upon my fingers?'

The AUDITIONERS *look at each other, then . . .*

HENRY. Carry on.

HENRIETTA. 'And – once you had dragged me back here to
the dull town of my birth some twenty summers previously –
how could you not have noticed that I made myself an agreeable circle of aquaintance.'

JENNY. Continue.

HENRIETTA. 'Which you have shattered with the news of your
intentions for my future, which as you recollect are for me to
marry Thomas Channing, grocer, someone whom I cannot
love?'

Slight pause. HENRIETTA *sits.*

HENRY. Splendid.

ELIZABETH MEECH. Dear Henrietta.

JENNY. I wonder, Miss Stickland, if you might consider taking
on / this role?

HENRIETTA. And does the defiant Mary marry 'Thomas
Channing, grocer'?

HENRY. Yes.

HENRIETTA. And then?

After a look between the AUDITIONERS.

JENNY. She puts poison in her husband's porridge, flees, but is
arrested, tried, condemned . . .

HENRY. . . . pleads her belly . . .

ELIZABETH MEECH. . . . her child is born and dragged from
her arms . . .

JENNY. . . . and she's burnt at the stake.

HENRIETTA. I see. Well, I'll consider it.

HENRY. You'll *consider it*?

WILLIAM. And no doubt whatever a-p-p-prehensions she may
have, she will p-p-prevail against them.

HENRIETTA (*standing and waving her sister to her feet*).
William, you are to do the play in order to develop your
capacities for social interaction, in order to impress a certain
party. Give me one good reason why I should have any other
interest in this enterprise?

*Enter four gorgeous – and gorgeously-attired – OFFICERS,
two from the German Heavy Dragoons and two from the
Royal Dragoons. They are* LIEUTENANT FREDERICK
BARON USLAU, CAPTAIN COUNT KIELMANREGGE,
MAJOR JAMES BRINE *and* CAPTAIN JOSEPH
HAGLEY.

USLAU. Is zis ver iz ze play?

HENRIETTA *and* MARY SUSANNAH *look, gasp, grab
each other's hands, and sit.*

BRINE. Looks like it, Lieutenant.

USLAU. Fraulein, ve are vrom ze barracks. My nem iz Lieutenant Frederick Baron Uslau. Und zis iz Captain Count
Kielmanregge.

MARY SUSANNAH. Baron?

HENRIETTA. Count?

JENNY. How do you do? And . . .

BRINE. Major James Brine, Royal Dragoons.

HAGLEY. Captain Hagley.

BRINE. We read your Bill.

JENNY. Well, as you know, we are seeking out performers for a
play . . .

HAGLEY. Performers?

HENRY. Actors . . .

The OFFICERS *look at each other, smiling and shaking their
heads.*

ELIZABETH MEECH. Singers . . .

JENNY. Dancers . . .

USLAU. Ah. Zertainly ve zing und dance.

> HAGLEY *has a musical instrument.*

KIELMANREGGE. But we do not dance alone. Particularly in ze presence of zuch charming ladies. Fräulein?

> KIELMANREGGE *takes* HENRIETTA*'s arm as* HAGLEY *starts to play.*

HENRIETTA. Charmed.

BRINE. May I have the pleasure?

MARY SUSANNAH. I . . . Delighted.

USLAU. Und, dear Fräulein . . .

ANN HAZARD. Uh . . .

> USLAU *looks to* HENRY, *who takes* CATHERINE *on to the floor. The four couples dance as* HAGLEY *starts to sing Richard Brinsley Sheridan's 'Here's to the Maiden of Bashful Fifteen'.*

HAGLEY.
> Here's to the maiden of bashful fifteen;
> Here's to the widow of fifty;
> Here's to the flaunting extravagant quean,
> And here's to the housewife that's thrifty.
>
> *Chorus*
> Let the toast pass,
> Drink to the lass,
> I'll warrant she'll prove an excuse for a glass.
>
> Here's to the charmer whose dimples we prize
> Now to the maid who has none, sir:
> Here's to the girl with a pair of blue eyes,
> And here's to the nymph with but one, sir.
> (*Chorus*)
>
> For let 'em be clumsy, or let 'em be slim,
> Young or ancient, I care not a feather;

So fill a pint bumper quite up to the brim,
And let us e'en toast them together.
(*Chorus*)

*As the dance proceeds, it is quickly apparent that while all
are good,* USLAU *and* ANN HAZARD *are spectacular.
Gradually the other couples move apart and stop dancing, to
watch their dramatic display.*

USLAU *and* ANN HAZARD's *big finish is followed by huge
applause. Once she has stopped dancing,* ANN HAZARD
looks like a little rabbit again.

USLAU. Fräulein. I am . . . overvelmed.

ANN HAZARD. I did . . . one winter . . . in Vienna . . .

ELIZABETH MEECH. Miss Hazard, we have found your true
vocation.

JOHN MANFIELD *stands in the doorway.*

JOHN MANFIELD. Ah, Mrs Manfield, there you are.

CATHERINE. Mr Manfield.

JOHN MANFIELD. We are due at the Shire Hall half an hour
ago.

CATHERINE. Not again.

JOHN MANFIELD (*whispering*). Mrs Manfield, I am the
Mayor of Dorchester.

CATHERINE. Mr Manfield, of this I am made constantly
aware.

ELIZABETH MEECH. Mr Mayor, we have detained your wife
on pressing business. Her singular talents make her vital to
this enterprise.

JENNY (*alarmed*). Um . . .

CATHERINE. Oh?

ELIZABETH MEECH. We're hoping she'll accept our invitation to oversee the wardrobe of the whole production.

CATHERINE. Ah.

JOHN MANFIELD. Well, I . . .

HENRY. A role which no one else could possibly perform.

ELIZABETH MEECH. Why only decorate yourself when you can decorate the stage!

CATHERINE. Indeed, my sense of style is often commented upon. I bid you all goodnight. Mr Manfield.

JOHN MANFIELD. As do I.

The MANFIELDS *leave*.

HENRY (*aside to* ELIZABETH MEECH). Graciously accomplished.

JENNY. Gentlemen, I hope we may persuade you also to participate in our entertainment.

BRINE (*with a bow to the* LADIES). Of course.

KIELMANREGGE. Naturally.

The LADIES *smile*.

HENRIETTA. We really should leave. Miss Meech, your sister will be quite agitated.

WILLIAM. Um, will my cousin . . . ?

MARY SUSANNAH. We will inform your cousin Mary you have taken this bold step as soon as we arrive.

USLAU. Miss Stickland, vould it be . . . Might ve ezcort you to your next engagement?

HENRIETTA. I'm sure we'd be delighted.

MARY SUSANNAH. William will pick up hints from their deportment.

HENRIETTA. And not just their deportment. Ada, do not imagine for an instant that I haven't seen you skulking there.

ADA GAPE. Sorry, Miss Henrietta.

She follows the STICKLANDS *and* OFFICERS *out.*

WILLIAM (*bitterly*). Deportment. Right.

He follows them out, as SUSANNAH *enters to clear up.*

ELIZABETH MEECH. An unexpectedly successful evening.

SUSANNAH. You'm done?

ELIZABETH MEECH *goes out.*

JENNY. Yes, thank you, Mrs Carter.

SUSANNAH. Well, I do hope to see you for the play-acting again. S'long as you settle up for this one, mind.

She goes out. JENNY *looks to* HENRY.

HENRY. I fear my father's adamant.

JENNY. I hope you will continue to assist us, nonetheless.

HENRY. I have already done so.

He holds up the audition speech. It is clear from the black lines across it that he has edited it heavily. Then he hands it to JENNY *to read.*

JENNY. 'Mother, you are absent through my childhood. You send me up to London and present me with a glittering jewel box which you slam shut on my fingers. You drag me back here, where I manage to make an agreeable circle of aquaintance. And now – *this*?'

She looks to HENRY.

It's better. I think we will work very well together.

HENRY. As you say, the theatre is a collaborative art.

HENRY *goes out, past an entering* YOUNG WOMAN, *whom he does not acknowledge.* JENNY *looks faintly surprised at this. Soft music.*

JENNY. Good evening. Do you come here for the play?

The YOUNG WOMAN *nods.*

I fear the auditions have finished for this evening.

The YOUNG WOMAN *shrugs and turns to go.*

But . . . But, you can come back another day.

YOUNG WOMAN (*turning back to* JENNY). Of course. I will.

Scene Three – 'Dear Miss Meech, it's just a play'

Tuesday 17th July. An evening whist party in MARIA's *upstairs apartment.* WOMEN *are playing whist. Table one:* EDITH FEAVER, LUCY FEAVER, ELEANOR, CHARLOTTE MEECH. *Table two:* FANNY STICKLAND, LUCIA, MARIA, PHYLLIS FRAMPTON. *Table three:* MARY STICKLAND, MARY FRAMPTON, HARRIET FRAMPTON *and* JANE. *Table four:* MAY SHERIDAN *and* ANNABELLE SHERIDAN, ROSEMARY CRUNDELL *and* LETITIA SOMNER. *There are four candles on each table, slowly burning away.* MAUD, MARIA's *servant, sits gloomily by the door.* MARY SHIRLEY *is bored of playing with her doll, and is loitering around her aunt,* MARY FRAMPTON. *A* MUSICIAN *sits in the corner, playing a cello.* MARY *sits apart from the rest, writing. Occasionally there is the cry of the night watchman. For a while the* WOMEN *play silently, then* . . .

MARIA. I'm all of a flummox. I know I shouldn't be, but it is, at the very least, unsettling.

MARY FRAMPTON. Dear Miss Meech, it's just a play.

MAY. It is, at the least, unsettling.

They play in silence.

JANE. Mr Stickland said over breakfast, that Mr Templeman was rather hostile to the venture.

LUCIA. I think my husband feels there are more important matters to address.

FANNY. Naturally there are always more important matters.

MARY. What's the French for 'honour'?

Slight pause.

LUCY. I think it's – '*honneur*'.

MARY STICKLAND. Darling, what are you writing?

MARY. A novella.

LUCY. Honestly?

MARY SHIRLEY. What's it about?

MARY. Well, it begins when this daring young blade is cap-
    tured by a gang of wicked brigands who imprison him in
    their stinking cellar and –

    LUCY*'s eyes have been getting wider and wider.* FANNY
    interrupts.

FANNY. Mother-in-law. How is your son William?

ELEANOR. Well . . .

    MARY *knows where this is going and responds in melodra-
    matic despair.*

MARY. Huh!

ELEANOR (*to* LUCY). No, Lucy!

MARY SHIRLEY. You must follow suit.

    Taking her cards.

    See?

LUCY. I thought I was. I can hardly see the pictures.

CHARLOTTE. Elizabeth had them sent from France.

FANNY. George is sure there won't be playing cards until this
    war is over.

PHYLLIS. The Corsican pig will come, but he will not take my
    Wollaston!

A little light laughter.

ELEANOR. So what's wrong with my son William?

HARRIET. He looked most charming at the Assize Ball.

ROSEMARY (*to* MARY SHIRLEY). It was your first ball, wasn't it, dear?

MARY SHIRLEY (*to* LUCY). *And* I danced with the Princesses.

She dances with her doll.

LETITIA. Such lovely fireworks.

MARIA. Ladies . . .

MAY. And you couldn't see them . . .

MARY FRAMPTON. . . . and so . . .

MARY SHIRLEY. . . . I was picked up by the King!

A flurry.

MARY MEECH. Do be quiet!

The MUSICIAN *stops. A moment, then the* WOMEN *play on.*

LETITIA. I do so love watching couples dancing.

The door flies open. MAUD *stands and announces.*

MAUD. Miss Meech. Miss Henrietta, Miss Mary Susannah.

HARRIET. Perhaps William should escort you to the next.

MARY. What is the French for, 'I would rather die'?

Trailed by MARY SUSANNAH *and* HENRIETTA, ELIZA-BETH MEECH *bursts into the room. They are in high spirits: it should feel as if the room has stopped holding its breath.* MARIA *concentrates hard on the game and affects not to notice the arrival of her sister.*

ELIZABETH MEECH. My dear child, I hope there'll be no need of that. Greetings to you all. Sister, I hope my late arrival hasn't upset the evening.

MARIA. Hardly noticed you were gone.

HENRIETTA. Are we too late for tea?

ELIZABETH MEECH looks to MARIA.

MARIA. The new maid you engaged is ill.

MAUD. 'Ill.'

ELIZABETH MEECH. In that case I shall make it.

She turns to go to the kitchen.

LUCIA. May we inquire if anyone attended the 'audition'?

HENRIETTA. There were some German officers.

ELIZABETH MEECH. Tea it is!

ELIZABETH MEECH exits.

MARY SUSANNAH. And, Mary, your charming distant cousin William . . .

MARY *(she's had enough)*. I shall see if Miss Meech needs help.

MARY flounces off into the kitchen, where ELIZABETH MEECH is lighting the stove and setting out the cups.

ROSEMARY *(to HENRIETTA)*. Darlings, do come here . . .

ELEANOR. . . . have a slice of cake.

JANE. And tell us all about the officers.

The lights dim on the chattering WOMEN and rise on the kitchen.

MARY. What happened to – Tilda?

ELIZABETH MEECH. Some crockery went missing. My sister went round to her house, and found her child, Rose, playing with our teapot.

Beat.

And the person who you'd rather die than dance with. Your distant cousin William?

MARY. I am sure he's very . . . eligible.

ELIZABETH MEECH. But that is . . . not enough?

MARY. I think . . .

ELIZABETH MEECH. I was your age once, Miss Stickland.

> *Slight pause.*

> Now, shall we make the tea . . . ?

MARY. What do you mean, my age?

> *Pause.*

> Do you mean, there was . . .

ELIZABETH MEECH (*dismissively, filling the kettle*). I mean . . . there was a young man. French. We met at Weymouth.

MARIA (*calls*). Elizabeth! Do hurry!

MARY. And did your sister know?

> ELIZABETH MEECH *decides to tell her.*

ELIZABETH MEECH. He asked me to go with him on the Newfoundland packet. To start a 'new life full of song'.

MARY. Full of song?

ELIZABETH MEECH. He used to sing a little, well, French lullaby.

As she puts the kettle on the stove, she sings a song with words taken from Thomas Hardy's 'The Return of the Native':

> *Le point du jour*
> *A nos bosquets*
> *rend toute leur parure;*
> *Flore est plus belle a son retour*
> *L'oiseau reprend doux chant d'amour;*
> *Tout celebre dans la nature*
> *Le point du jour.*

MARY. And then?

ELIZABETH MEECH (*raises her hand to silence her*). We arranged to meet at dawn. I packed a small brown suitcase, put on my best white gloves and walked down to the port.

MARY. You're going to say he wasn't there.

ELIZABETH MEECH. Oh, he was there.

Beat.

He was sitting at the bottom of a flight of steps watching seagulls. I took the first step towards him. But suddenly a feeling raced through me and each step became the face of my mother, my brother Giles, Maria.

MARY. What became of him?

ELIZABETH MEECH. If only he'd turned round . . .

MARY. Unrequited love. How wonderful.

ELIZABETH MEECH. Is it?

ELIZABETH MEECH *looks around her kitchen.*

Truly?

MARY. Dear Miss Meech. Elizabeth.

MARY *embraces* ELIZABETH MEECH. *The water boils.*

ELIZABETH MEECH (*gathering herself, filling the pot*). Now, come. Let's tend to my sister.

She picks up the tray and walks towards the living room. As ELIZABETH MEECH *and* MARY *walk into the room:*

MARY STICKLAND. You say that he was a baron?

HENRIETTA. And the other was a count.

JANE. Then it's settled. I shall book us all front-row seats.

MAY. I shall wear my peacock-blue dress.

ANNABELLE. But, sister, in London, they're wearing Egyptian brown.

MARY FRAMPTON. Do you suppose the company of actors is quite full?

MARIA. Ladies, I really must / insist –

MARY SUSANNAH. I think not.

CHARLOTTE. My husband Giles has always said it was a choice between the cloth and, um . . .

EDITH. . . . the boards.

ELEANOR. And William will give the performance of his life!

MARY. I think I should like to go home.

MARY STICKLAND (*standing*). Of course, dear.

MARY. No, Mother, there is no need for you to come.

MARY STICKLAND. But, dear . . .

MARY. And now Miss Elizabeth is home, perhaps you can settle to the game.

MARY *leaves*.

ELIZABETH MEECH (*to the* MUSICIAN). Something cheery.

MARIA (*gesturing her to sit*). Elizabeth . . . ?

ELIZABETH MEECH (*not sitting*). Miss Frampton, did I hear you express an interest in the play?

MARIA *shakes her head. The game resumes. The* CHORUS *appear to lead us into the next scene.*

CHORUS. And with but five minutes wanting of half past nine o'clock,

– Miss Stickland hastened out into the sticky summer night.

– And at the Shambles entrance stood a coachman, to whom Miss Stickland furnished a small coin,

– requesting that he take her instantly to a public house outside of the town.

– 'You be quite sure, miss?'

– asked the coachman, wary of the address.

– 'Oh yes, indeed',

– said the bold young lady, seating herself in the carriage, and turning her head firmly towards the Weymouth Road.

– At last she found her destination, but to her dismay its blistered door was locked and barred.

– But through a crack she saw the flicker of a shadow

– and she heard a muffled cry.

Scene Four – 'We prefer we do be called 'Free Traders'

The Crown Inn. The wedding party of EMMANUEL CHARLES *and the heavily pregnant* ELIZABETH HARDY, *she in her wedding dress. The guests include:* OLD ISAAC, *his elderly mother* PEG, *his son* ISAAC GULLIVER, *and his sisters* ANN CRAWFORD, LIZZIE FRYER *and* HANNAH SILLER; LOVEY WARNE, CASSANDRA PLOUGHMAN, FRENCH PETER, BESSIE CATCHPOLE, BILLY COOMBS, KATIE PRESTON *and her brood* TIM, TOM, SAM, BOB *and* NIPPER. *There are four little smuggler bridesmaids,* MEG, POPPET, EMILY *and* ANNIE; *a grumpy smuggler pageboy called* HERBERT. *One reason why* HERBERT *is grumpy is that his* SISTERS – *eager to practice their knots – keep tying him up.*

We arrive at the beginning of a song based on the contemporary air 'Valparaiso Round the Horn'. During the song, the CHILDREN *act out the happy couple and their adventures.*

ALL EXCEPT CHARLESES.
    So who are we and why are we assembled?

ALL OTHERS.
    Free traders to a man and to a gal! (To a gal.)

With much pointing at LIZZIE, ANN CRAWFORD *and* OLD GULLIVER.

Though to their pa a bidder diserppointment (diserppoint-
    ment)
Old Gulliver's two gals are here as well! (Here as well).

Chorus
What's in your drawers? (in your drawers)
What's in yours? (what's in yours?)
'Tis a secret as we're not inclined to tell.
For all kind of contrabandin'll be landin'
Now the happy couple's rung the nuptual bell!
For we be here to celebrate a wedding (a wedding)
The finest pairs of owlers in the land (land, land)
They met a-top the dizzy cliffs of Lulworth (Lulworth) –

The song is interrupted by a tap on the window. Everyone stops. Whispering.

ANN CRAWFORD. Who's that?

FRENCH PETER. I'll take a gander.

TIM. I'll go.

He goes out.

OLD GULLIVER. We 'specting folk?

TIM (*offstage*). Be a speck little body.

LOVEY (*shouts*). This be a private party.

Re-enter TIM *with* MARY.

ELIZABETH HARDY. Your business?

HANNAH. Speak, speak!

MARY. I was looking for . . . a Mr Gulliver.

OLD GULLIVER. And what do you a-want wi' me?

MARY. Uh . . .

ISAAC. Mary, 'tis fine.

HANNAH. 'Mary'?

MARY. Isaac.

LIZZIE. 'Isaac'?

MARY. You told me, The Crown Inn, any evening . . .

ISAAC (*trying to take her aside*). Yes I did. But . . .

MEG. Who's the pretty miss?

OLD GULLIVER. Now, Isaac, bain't you going to introduce us?

ISAAC. Mary, I'd like you to meet Father. Who as I say be . . .
be a publican.

MARY. I'm very pleased to . . .

EMMANUEL. Likewise, Mary . . . ?

MARY. Stickland.

OLD GULLIVER. Likewise even more.

He shakes her hand.

ISAAC. And my sister, Lizzie . . .

LIZZIE. Charmed.

ISAAC. Ann, my sister, who be married to a fine doctor . . .

LOVEY (*singing a line from the song*).
    Though to their pa a bidder diserppointment . . .

ELIZABETH HARDY. Shh.

OLD GULLIVER (*prompting, to cover*). The lovely Miss
Warne . . .

ISAAC. Thank you, Father . . . Miss Lovey Warne and Miss
Siller.

OLD GULLIVER. Who are . . .

ISAAC. Who are . . .

PEG. . . . dear family friends.

OLD GULLIVER. And French Peter –

ISAAC. That's Mr Peter French, the noted . . .

PEG. . . . table polisher.

OLD GULLIVER. And of course, the happy couple whose nuptuals we do celebrate this evening . . .

CASSANDRA. And not a day too soon.

MARY (*disappointed*). But I thought you said they were the White Wigs, 'the most fearless smugglers' band in Dorsetshire'.

Terrible pause.

Isn't one of you the finest female shot in all the kingdom?

LOVEY *takes out a pistol, swirls it round, and puts it away.*

LOVEY. And so I be.

OLD GULLIVER. We prefer we do be called 'Free Traders'.

Slight pause.

PEG. Now, my boy, make Miss Stickland welcome.

KATIE. How about a glass of fine French wine?

BESSIE. Or a cup of rare green tea.

LIZZIE (*taking* MARY*'s arm*). And she can tell us where, when, why . . .

ANN CRAWFORD. . . . and how . . .

LIZZIE. . . . she do meet our vooty brother.

MARY. Well, 'when' . . . Was it four weeks ago?

ISAAC *nods despairingly.*

MARY. Where, along the coast – I was riding to Lulworth Cove. Why? To give Udolpho a good run. How? It was bitten by a . . .

HERBERT. A wasp?

MARY. No, a horse-fly, and she reared.

MEG. And you were flounced off . . .

SAM. . . . like a floppy mummet-doll.

ISAAC. No, but she bolted, and as I was riding by, I rode aside and took the bridle and slowed her down, and that was that.

EMILY (*to* MARY). He do save your life?

MARY. I thought he was a foreigner.

ANN CRAWFORD. That'll be his diddycoy look.

LIZZIE. That'll be his hair.

ISAAC. *Mais Oui*.

ELIZABETH HARDY. Did you say, the cliffs at Lulworth Cove?

CASSANDRA. She did.

LOVEY. 'Tis just where we leaves off.

OLD GULLIVER. High time to pick it up again.

BOB (*smacking pans together*). One, two –

TIM/SAM/TOM/NIPPER. One, two, three, four . . .

   The song continues.

ALL EXCEPT CHARLESES.
      We'm meeting here to celebrate a wedding (a wedding)
      The finest pairs of owlers in the land (land, land)
      They met a-top the dizzy cliffs of Lulworth (Lulworth)
      With some vital nightal business all at hand (all at hand).
      (*Chorus*)

      There's silk and rum and baccy being landed (landed),
      There's a lugger bobbing lively on the main (the main).
      And as he races up with his last load, like (load, like),
      There's a cry of:

TIM/SAM/TOM/NIPPER/ANNIE.
      Stop there in King George's Name! (name, name).

ALL EXCEPT CHARLESES.
>   (*Chorus*)
>   She do jump into the waggon with their booty (booty)
>   But the excise men are gaining on them fast (fast, fast).
>   And he says: Take off your dress and double quick now
>   (quick now),
>   And she says: Sir, I'm not that kind of lass (lass, lass).
>   (*Chorus*)
>
>   So he wraps the bolt o'silk around her belly (her belly),
>   And puts a heavy greatcoat on the top (top, top).
>   And when the men arrive they finds a mammy (a
>   mammy),
>   And a daddy with a babe about to pop (pop, pop)!
>   (*Chorus*)

Wild applause. Then the music turns ghostie-ghoulie.

LOVEY. Well, I say she'd a-been a-better doing it running off into the furse and making out to be a ghost or ghoulie.

TOM/SAM/BOB/NIPPER/ANNIE. Oooooh . . .

EMMANUEL. Oh, Miss Lovey Warne.

LOVEY. You don't even need a ghostie, all you want's the rattle of dead bones.

TOM/SAM/BOB/NIPPER/ANNIE. Aarrgh . . .

BESSIE. . . . or the clanking of a chain . . .

PEG. . . . or a scream in the middle in the night –

The door flies open. EVERYBODY's weapons – guns and swords and daggers – flash out. A boy called BILLY LAWRENCE runs in.

BILLY. Help me! Hide me! Or I'll . . . Ah.

He picks up that the room is full of heavily armed people.

HENRY BUSH (*offstage*). Boy! Billy-boy! Stop! Come back here!

BILLY (*to* MARY). Please.

TIM. Quick!

SAM. Over here!

NIPPER. Under . . .

MARY. Uh . . . under the table?

HENRY BUSH (*offstage but closer*). Billy Lawrence! Come back here or I'll have the skin off your back!

BILLY scuttles under the table. The weapons disappear as quickly as they came, and everyone reconfigures themselves as a group of people having a quiet evening in the pub, as normal as can be.

(*Still offstage.*) Billy!

HENRY BUSH *enters, with a lantern.*

Billy, where are you?

ELIZABETH HARDY. May we help you?

HENRY BUSH. Do a boy come by here?

OLD GULLIVER. What manner of child?

HENRY BUSH. A scruffy little feller, 'bout so high.

OLD GULLIVER. Do anyone of you see a little feller, 'bout so, about this high?

Murmurs between each other. Shaking of heads.

CASSANDRA. Seems not.

MEG *pushes forward the sullen-looking* HERBERT.

MEG. You could take him, if you've a mind.

HERBERT *scowls at* MEG *and pulls himself free.*

EMMANUEL. So what be your interest in the child?

HENRY BUSH. His father do send him to me to work as my apprentice, like. But he do only work a half a day afore he's off . . .

CASSANDRA. Tut tut.

HANNAH. Young folks nowadays.

OLD GULLIVER. Now, we would offer you summat warm, like, to keep out the cold . . .

PEG. But I reckon as he'll be wanting to keep on looking.

HENRY BUSH. True enough.

Slight pause.

Well, if you see him . . . my name's Henry Bush. Of Mill Street, Fordington.

ELIZABETH HARDY. We'll surely let you know.

HENRY BUSH *goes out. A pause.* FRENCH PETER *closes the door. Attention on the table.* HERBERT *pulls the tablecloth and* BILLY *crawls out.*

OLD GULLIVER. Now I be speculating, as for why a vooty boy, 'prentice like to a fine master with a fine trade, takes it in his head to run away?

LOVEY. Maybe he misses his mama.

HANNAH. Why not run to her then?

BILLY. Well, I . . . Like, I . . . I allus dream, like, of going for a sailor.

FRENCH PETER. Well, you come to the right place if you wants for seawork.

BILLY. And to do my service for King George!

A silence.

OLD GULLIVER. Now mebbe you've not come to the right place.

ANN CRAWFORD. But, surely, if the lad needs to bed down for the night . . .

LIZZIE (*to* ELIZABETH HARDY). He can sweep out and wash up, can't he?

ELIZABETH HARDY. Surely can.

EMMANUEL. Only for one night, mind.

> OLD GULLIVER *hands* BILLY *his glass.* BILLY *smiles, picks up a tray, takes* OLD GULLIVER*'s glass and starts to collect other glasses.*

CASSANDRA. Bidden this a wedding? Bidden there to be dancing?

> *Cheers, music and people take to the floor.*

EMMANUEL (*to* ELIZABETH HARDY). May I have the pleasure?

BILLY COOMBS (*to* KATIE). My dear?

LOVEY (*to* FRENCH PETER). Come on, you.

> MARY *and* ISAAC *have a quiet word as the others dance.*

MARY. You did say, 'any evening'.

ISAAC. I had a mind you wouldn't come.

MARY. I was writing you a letter.

ISAAC. So this t'aint our last encounter?

MARY. My family must never know.

ISAAC. Pa says, 'concealment is better than injury'.

MARY. There is a play. For which anybody can volunteer.

ISAAC. In my line of work, we'm famous for disguise.

MARY. Presumably I can't call you Mr Gulliver.

ISAAC. No. *Puis-je danser avec toi?*

MARY. Only if you promise me, that when we look back and remember this . . . you will remember I danced well.

ISAAC. *Enchanté.*

She takes him by the arm and joins him in the dancing. She isn't very good. The dance swirls and grows; through the couples dances the YOUNG WOMAN *who we saw at the end of the audition. The* SMUGGLERS *melt away and she is left dancing alone.*

Scene Five – 'I wonder, is this quite appropriate?'

We are in Maumbury Rings, the arena-shaped earthwork on the outskirts of Dorchester, on the hot, bright mid afternoon of Saturday 11th August. The YOUNG WOMAN *dances round the Rings.* JENNY *enters with her script, and watches the* YOUNG WOMAN *dancing. The* YOUNG WOMAN *stops. Her music continues until she goes.*

JENNY. Please, don't stop.

YOUNG WOMAN. I was waiting for you . . .

JENNY. Such a hot afternoon for dancing. You can imagine how the gladiators felt, when Maumbury Rings was a Roman amphitheatre.

YOUNG WOMAN. You are meeting here today.

JENNY. We are having difficulties in finding places to rehearse.

The YOUNG WOMAN *turns away, to look across the Rings, to where* ACTORS *in the play are already assembling, including* ISAAC, *who is setting out chairs for a trial scene.* JENNY *thinks the* YOUNG WOMAN *is going. To stop her:*

Today we are doing Judge Jeffreys' Bloody Assize but tomorrow I need people for the Mary Channing wedding scene. You know this is where they burnt her?

YOUNG WOMAN. Broke her neck.

JENNY. Yes, of course, to save her suffering. That was their idea of mercy, a hundred years ago. May I take your name?

By now REVERAND GILES MEECH *and* CHARLOTTE, HENRY, ELIZABETH MEECH, CATHERINE *with a roll of drawings,* JOHN FEAVER *and* EDITH *and their daughter* LUCY, CAROLINE HINGE, BOWER, *and* ANN HAZARD *have assembled.* CATHERINE *puts a wig on* GILES. JENNY*'s attention is taken by a grave-faced* USLAU, *who has entered also.*

USLAU. Fräulein Hodge?

JENNY (*turning to him*). Ah, Baron. Thank goodness, this is your big scene. But, where is Count Kielmanregge?

USLAU. Fräulein Hodge, he iz not here.

JENNY. Baron, this is the third week of rehearsal . . .

USLAU. Fräulein Hodge, our regiment iz posted.

JENNY. Posted? When?

USLAU. Zis very afternoon. In twenty minutes we go to Radypool in Weymouth.

JENNY. What?

USLAU *goes out. The* YOUNG WOMAN *has disappeared.* GILES *and* CHARLOTTE *and* CATHERINE *are bearing down on* JENNY, *as* ROBERT *enters with* JANE, MARY SUSANNAH *and* HENRIETTA, MARY, WILLIAM, *and* MARY FRAMPTON, *and* ADA GAPE.

GILES. Miss Hodge. We are to rehearse out here? In this awesome heat?

JENNY. Well, we were . . .

GILES. In this wig?

CATHERINE. What's wrong with it?

CHARLOTTE. I think my husband fears the effect upon his constitution . . .

HENRIETTA *nudges* WILLIAM. ISAAC *clocks this conversation.*

HENRIETTA. William, a chair, please . . .

MARY SUSANNAH (*also nudging* WILLIAM). For your
distant cousin Mary . . .

HENRIETTA. And perhaps a parasol . . .

CATHERINE. Speaking of wigs, Miss Hodge, I have brought
the costume drawings for the Mary Channing wedding party,
as you asked me.

JENNY. Splendid.

> MARY *attracts* ISAAC's *attention*.

MARY. Good evening, Mr – Swift?

ISAAC. Yours to command, Miss – Stickland?

> *Having picked up a chair,* WILLIAM *sees* MARY *is
> engaged. He stands there a moment or two, before putting it
> down, to* HENRIETTA *and* MARY SUSANNAH's *despair*.

CATHERINE. But I must own that due to the current shortage
of materials, I have no idea how they may be realised.
Unless you would like Mary Channing married in a sack.

JENNY. Yes. Mrs Manfield . . .

> HENRY *and* ELIZABETH MEECH *approach*.

HENRY. Miss Hodge. The courtroom is set out by the indispen-
sible Mr Swift.

JENNY. Yes, thanks so much, Mr . . .

ELIZABETH MEECH. However, once again, it seems the
German Officers have failed us . . .

JENNY. I fear their absence will be permanent.

> *Enough people have heard this for a sudden silence to fall on
> the* COMPANY.

HENRY. I beg your pardon?

HENRIETTA. What?

JENNY. Their regiment is posted.

HENRIETTA (*aghast*). And their return to Dorchester?

BOWER. Miss Stickland, the German officers serve in the King's Own Heavy Dragoons. Bonaparte could land his troops at any place in southern England.

CAROLINE HINGE. They could be posted anywhere at any time.

HENRY looks questioningly to ELIZABETH MEECH.

ELIZABETH MEECH. Colonel William Bower. Miss Hinge's . . . friend.

CATHERINE. One hopes they are better timekeepers on the drilling square.

HENRY looks to JENNY, who gives a gesture of wild despair. ISAAC has been looking in the prompt script.

ISAAC. Miss Hodge?

JENNY. Mr Swift.

ISAAC. I do think you'll find . . .

JENNY. What?

ISAAC. You do have nearly everyone for the Mary Channing wedding scene.

He shows her the book.

JENNY. We do. Thank you so much, Mr Swift. Miss Henrietta Stickland, Mr William Stickland . . . and although Major Brine is absent on manoeuvres . . . Mr Meech can play Mary Channing's former sweetheart, Jack.

GILES removes his wig. HENRY and ISAAC reset the chairs. As she hands scripts round, ELIZABETH MEECH has noticed that the rehearsal is developing an audience of LABOURERS, sitting on the banks of the Rings. This includes EDWARD FUDGE and TOM CHAFFLEY and JANEY CHAFFLEY.

HENRY. We'll use this table, and if we can have three chairs here, here and here.

GILES (*looking at his script*). So my cue is ' . . . my aquaintance.' I say – 'Certainly.'

JENNY. Correct.

ADA GAPE *realises that* HENRIETTA *has not moved since hearing the news about the Germans.*

ADA GAPE. Be you alright, miss?

HENRIETTA (*taking out a patterned hankerchief*). Take this to the captain. Quickly.

ADA GAPE *rushes out with the hankerchief, as:*

GILES (*reading his lines*). ' . . . I please.' 'Hear, hear.' ' . . . father-in-law!' 'As is obviously right and proper!'

JENNY. And the bridegroom's parents . . . Mr Feaver and, ah, Mrs Feaver, would you please be Mrs Channing . . .

EDITH *giggles in terror.*

JOHN FEAVER. Uh, in fact, my wife does not care to . . .

HENRY. She is entirely silent in this scene.

JENNY. And everybody else is wedding guests . . .

ELIZABETH MEECH. Uh, Colonel Bower?

BOWER (*with a glance at* CAROLINE HINGE). Well, indeed.

GILES. ' . . . my childhood confidante.' 'Why not?' ' . . . good Tom the fiddler!' 'As is clearly suitable.'

HENRY (*waving at the characters*). Our situation is this. The young and wayward Mary Brooks' parents – played by Mr and Mrs Robert Stickland – have decided she must marry Thomas Channing, grocer. After the ceremony, the parents of the bride and groom return home for a small and private party. Miss Feaver, you're a bridesmaid. And . . .

HENRIETTA *is standing a little apart, looking mournfully off to where* ADA GAPE *departed.*

Miss Stickland, the bride has returned already, you go there.

Still distant, HENRIETTA *allows herself to be placed in the scene.*

JENNY. And if you, Mr . . . Meech would sit beside Miss Stickland, and maybe take her hand . . .

GILES *gives a quizzical look.*

HENRY. . . . she has just been married.

JENNY. And the rest of the main bridal party, enter.

HENRY. To discover a scene of voluptuous abandon.

JANE. I enter here?

HENRY. The bridegroom's father speaks.

JOHN FEAVER. 'Pray, who and what is this?'

HENRY. And then, Miss Stickland . . .

HENRIETTA. Oh, I'm sorry . . .

HENRY (*showing her her cue and line in her script*). You speak after ' . . . what is this?'. Your line is 'It is my friends . . . '

HENRIETTA. Yes, yes, of course.

JENNY. Once more, Mr Feaver.

JOHN FEAVER. 'Pray, who and what is this?'

HENRIETTA. 'They are my friends. It is my wedding feast.'

JENNY. With perhaps more spirit, Miss Stickland.

HENRIETTA (*crossly*). 'They are my friends! It is my wedding feast!'

ROBERT. 'It appears to be everyone in Dorchester.'

HENRIETTA. 'Oh, Father, on my wedding day, I am surely permitted to share my joy with my aquaintance!'

GILES. 'Certainly.'

JOHN FEAVER. 'Mr Brook, when we said that we would be happy to divide up the expense . . . '

HENRY. And Miss Stickland kisses her dear –

WILLIAM. 'Mary, I wonder, is this quite right and p-p-p-proper . . . '

HENRIETTA. 'It is my wedding! I shall kiss anyone I please!'

GILES. 'Hear, hear!'

HENRIETTA. 'For instance, I shall kiss my dear father-in-law!'

GILES. 'As is obviously right and proper!'

JENNY. And you do . . .

HENRIETTA goes and kisses JOHN FEAVER decorously.

HENRIETTA. 'I shall kiss my dear sweet Nell, my childhood confidante . . . '

GILES. 'Why not?'

HENRY. And that's your sister.

HENRIETTA kisses MARY SUSANNAH.

HENRIETTA. 'And I shall kiss good Tom the fiddler!'

GILES. 'As is clearly suitable.'

JENNY. Which is obviously Mr Swift . . .

WILLIAM. 'You know this p-p-p-person?'

HENRIETTA kisses ISAAC absent-mindedly. ISAAC looks to MARY apologetically. MARY smiles and rolls her eyes.

HENRY. With a bit more passion, if you would, Miss Stickland.

HENRIETTA (*checking the script*). Oh, yes.

She throws her arms round ISAAC and kisses him more passionately. MARY folds her arms and bites her bottom lip. GILES rises.

GILES. Miss Hodge . . .

JENNY. Yes, Mr Meech?

GILES. I wonder, is this quite appropriate?

JENNY. Is what appropriate?

GILES. From the document you handed me, I was not aware that 'as is right and proper' and 'as is clearly suitable' referred to a married woman kissing and embracing half of Dorchester!

JENNY. Well, it is what occured.

ELIZABETH MEECH. Giles, it is a well-known story . . .

GILES. And you do not think that this will encourage similar behaviour in suggestible young people?

MARY SUSANNAH. Oh, I hardly think so.

The COMPANY *look at her in surprise.*

Seeing as she has a lover and poisons her new husband and ends up at the stake. Here.

GILES. May I see the play? The whole play?

ELIZABETH MEECH. Brother . . .

HENRY *hands over the script, as . . .*

ROBERT. Henrietta, did you say you had read this play?

HENRIETTA. Well, yes . . .

ROBERT. And did you show it to your mother?

GILES. Where . . . ?

HENRY (*bowing to the inevitable*). Page eighty-three.

MARY. I thought we should always listen to our mothers, Henrietta.

GILES. 'Scene Ten. The Trial of Mary Channing.'

He turns some pages.

For poisoning her husband. In which she speaks 'forcefully',
'defiantly', 'heroically'. 'Your honour, I ask you, if you were
a woman, forced into such a dull and dour marriage, would
you act differently?' And so on.

ROBERT. What's this?

GILES. I would say, this is not so much a cautionary tale, as an
advertisement!

JENNY. Well, actually . . .

She stops herself.

GILES. 'Well, actually' . . . ?

JENNY. The Judge did say she conducted a masterly defence.

GILES. Mr Stickland, I cannot believe that you will allow your
daughter to continue in the role of an adulteress and mur-
deress. However 'masterly' and 'heroic' she may be!

He almost flings the whole script back to HENRY, *as* ADA
GAPE *enters with the undelivered hankerchief, waving it
nervously at the distraught* HENRIETTA.

ROBERT. Yes, indeed . . . Henrietta?

HENRIETTA. It's all right, Papa. I have no more interest in this
loathsome play! Ada!

She rushes out, followed by ADA GAPE.

JANE. Oh, Henrietta.

She follows. ROBERT *is following her but is called back.*

HENRY. Mr Stickland. May I say a word?

ROBERT. Yes, what?

HENRY. The greatest drama is about the gap between what we
want in life and what we can achieve.

ROBERT. Oh, is that so?

MARY. Mary Channing had ambition for the kind of life she
wanted that went way beyond what her parents wanted for her.

ELIZABETH MEECH. Or was even possible, for a woman of her time.

GILES. Of any time!

HENRY. Her husband paid the price for that ambition. But so did she.

ROBERT. Yes, well . . . As long as . . . I must find my wife and daughter.

GILES. I will accompany you, Mr Stickland. Charlotte.

He turns to his wife.

CHARLOTTE. Then I will see you at the rectory.

GILES. Ah . . . yes.

He looks to his sister ELIZABETH MEECH, *who shrugs, as if to say, 'Go if you want to.'* WILLIAM *isn't sure what to do.*

ELIZABETH MEECH. Good evening, brother.

ROBERT. Miss Meech.

The LABOURERS *react with interest to the name 'Meech'.*

MARY SUSANNAH. William. Miss Stickland will need escorting home.

GILES *goes out.* WILLIAM *has a go, as* JENNY *speaks to* MARY.

WILLIAM (*to* MARY). Miss Stickland, may I have the honour –

JENNY. Miss Stickland, we have lost our Mary Channing.

CATHERINE. Miss Hodge, perhaps I could myself / essay the role . . .

JENNY (*to* MARY). I wonder if you might take it on?

MARY (*with a glance at* ISAAC). I would be delighted.

A smattering of applause. WILLIAM *shrugs to* MARY SUSANNAH *as, pressed by* TOM CHAFFLEY *and* JANEY, EDWARD *walks forward and interrupts.*

TOM CHAFFLEY. You be Miss Meech?

EDITH (*gesturing at* ELIZABETH MEECH). No, I . . .

ELIZABETH MEECH. I am Miss Meech.

BOWER. What do you want with her?

JANEY *nudges* EDWARD.

EDWARD. Just to tell 'er as my young Tilda sends her best regards. And to say as how she's doing fine and dandy where she's placed now.

ELIZABETH MEECH. Oh, and where is that?

BOWER. Miss Meech, do you know this man?

EDWARD. Dorchester Prison. Where d'you think she might be, after what you does to she?

ELIZABETH MEECH *raises her finger to stop* BOWER.

ELIZABETH MEECH. Uh, you are – Matilda Sibley's father?

EDWARD. That I be.

JANEY. Mr Edward Fudge.

ELIZABETH MEECH. Mr Fudge. Your daughter was dismissed from our employ for stealing.

EDWARD. All her little 'un do want is just to play, like, with a teapot.

JANEY. The child get a maggot in her head, to sup tea from a fancy china pot.

EDWARD. She's a whim for to be a fine kind lady. Just like you be.

EDWARD *turns away.* JANEY *and* TOM CHAFFLEY *walk away too, but singing an insulting, scarecrow ditty, which they keep up through the following dialogue.*

CHAFFLEYS.
    Where be that blackbird?
    I know where 'ee be

He be up in yonder tree
And I be after 'ee!
If I sees en, beggared
If I don't get in
Wi' a girt big stick I'll knock en down,
Blackbird, I'll 'ave 'ee!

HENRY. Miss Hodge, it is impossible to rehearse here.

JENNY. Yes. But what is the alternative?

HENRY. I am joint owner of the theatre with my father, and whatever his views, I am quite adamant that you shall . . . that we shall rehearse.

JENNY. 'We'?

HENRY. Yes, we.

To everyone.

Make your way to the theatre in North Square.

The CHAFFLEYS cheer. Everyone leaves except for ISAAC, MARY and CATHERINE. ISAAC is helping CATHERINE collect the costumes and her drawings.

CATHERINE. Well, congratulations.

MARY. Miss Manfield, on the question of the costumes . . .

CATHERINE. Yes?

MARY. I know someone . . . who might be able to assist.

CATHERINE. You do?

ISAAC. I be sure that cannot be the case, Miss Stickland.

MARY. He could obtain anything we wanted.

CATHERINE. Well, certainly, that sounds a most appealing proposition.

ISAAC. Take care, Miss Stickland, do not raise Mrs Manfield's hopes too high.

MARY (*looking directly at* ISAAC). All I am proposing is that this man might assist us, for the sake of something on which we've both set our hearts.

CATHERINE *turns and goes*.

ISAAC. In that case, 'tis likely as he will.

Scene Six – 'I should not be doing this'

The CHORUS *appears, putting cloaks on* MARY *and* ISAAC *and handing them spades*.

CHORUS. And five days later,

- a few miles south of Dorchester

- near the junction with the Bridport Road,

- at midnight,

- Mary Stickland finds herself engaged in a most unexpected

- and unladylike

- activity.

An unexpected amount of moonlight falls on ISAAC *and* MARY *digging in the earth.* MARY *wears* ISAAC's *great-coat.*

ISAAC. I should not be a-doing this.

MARY. Shh. You've done this many times before.

ISAAC. I should not be doing this with a young lady who do skim down a tree outside her window. And if her absence be detected, 'll have me lashed to the whipping cart.

MARY. It's an adventure.

ISAAC. Particular, by the light of the full moon.

MARY. Why not?

A VOICE *booms from offstage.*

VOICE. Halloa! Halloa!

ISAAC (*despairing*). *That's* why not.

A LARGE MAN *enters.*

LARGE MAN. Good evening!

ISAAC. So it be.

LARGE MAN. But even so . . . a strange time to be working in the fields, what what?

ISAAC. So it be.

LARGE MAN. Then may I inquire what in God's name you are doing?

ISAAC. We be . . . digging!

LARGE MAN. As I observe. Why are you digging?

ISAAC. We be digging . . .

MARY. . . . irrigation trenches, sir.

ISAAC. We be experimenting with a . . . novel system for . . .

MARY. . . . the provision of a constant supply of water . . .

ISAAC. . . . to an area of land.

Slight pause.

LARGE MAN. Go on.

ISAAC. Uh . . .

MARY. You see we think it's – it be possible, if we so construct the hedgerows that this – be – the lowest point of the field, we will perhaps discover that water which the land has not – uh – drunk, runs down and gathers here . . .

ISAAC. . . . whereupon it be my plan to gather up the waters and transport them – uh – by means of . . .

MARY. . . . pipes.

ISAAC. Pipes, yes, and . . .

MARY. . . . pumps.

ISAAC. Pumps, certainly, to a nearby mead, for to water a whole system of – um, nearby meads, a-going round, like.

LARGE MAN. Hm. Why must you do this in the dark?

Pause.

ISAAC *and* MARY. Because . . .

MARY. Because, my husband . . .

Enter the PRINCESSES AUGUSTA, MARY, *and* SOPHIA, *followed by ladies-in-waiting* ELIZABETH WALDEGRAVE *and* CAROLINE WALDEGRAVE, *and* FITZROY.

PRINCESS AUGUSTA. Oh, Papa, there you are.

ISAAC (*in a whisper to* MARY). *Mary.*

KING GEORGE (*for it is he*). Yes, here I am, what what?

PRINCESS MARY. You mustn't wander off in the middle of the night.

PRINCESS AUGUSTA. In the middle of the countryside.

PRINCESS SOPHIA. Mama was worried.

KING GEORGE. Yes, where is the Queen?

ISAAC *and* MARY *look at each other.*

FITZROY. She is in the carriage, sir.

KING GEORGE (*hearing a loud German voice approaching*). You are mistaken, Fitzroy. She is here!

Enter QUEEN CHARLOTTE, *followed by* GARTH.

QUEEN CHARLOTTE. *Ihre Majestät – wo sind Sie? Es ist nach Mitternacht! Wir sind erst dreiviertel des Weges von Bridport gekommen und noch mehrere Meilen von Wymouth entfernt!* [Your Majesty, where are you? It is past midnight!

We are yet but three quarters of the way from Bridport! We are still several miles from Weymouth!]

KING GEORGE. Yes, Madam. I was waiting for the wheel to be remounted.

QUEEN CHARLOTTE. *Das Wagenrad ist wieder angebracht! Sie sind es, der jetzt aufsteigen soll!* [The wheel is remounted! The person who must now remount is you!]

KING GEORGE (*to* ISAAC *and* MARY). Now I am told the person who must now remount is me. What what?

ELIZABETH WALDEGRAVE. Who are these people?

CAROLINE WALDEGRAVE. Digging, in the middle of the night?

QUEEN CHARLOTTE. *Sind es Spione von Bonaparte?* [Are they spies of Bonaparte?]

KING GEORGE. No, they are not spies of Bonaparte. They are my faithful and productive subjects. Now where are we? Blandford? Dorchester?

GARTH. No, sir. We were in Bridport.

QUEEN CHARLOTTE. *Wir werden nächste Woche nach Dorchester gehen um noch mehr Ihrer Dragonen zu mustern!* [We go to Dorchester next week! To review more of your Dragoons!]

CAROLINE WALDEGRAVE. As Her Majesty points out, you visit Dorchester next week, sir.

ELIZABETH WALDEGRAVE. To inspect your troops, and to visit the Earl of Dorchester at Came for a cold collation.

KING GEORGE. Well, yes, of course. Well, bustle, bustle. We must be up betimes for bathing, what?

MARY. Goodnight, Your Majesties.

KING GEORGE. Good fortune with your innovation, Mr –

ISAAC *and* MARY. Swift.

KING GEORGE. And Mrs Swift. Goodnight.

He goes out, followed by GARTH *and* FITZROY.

QUEEN CHARLOTTE (*to her* DAUGHTERS). *Komm, komm, beeilt euch!* [Come, come, no lingering.]

Provocatively, PRINCESS SOPHIA *looks questioningly at her mother, who repeats her instruction in English, with a heavy German accent.*

Augusta, Mary und Sophia, no lingering I zay!

QUEEN CHARLOTTE *goes out, followed by* CAROLINE WALDEGRAVE *and* ELIZABETH WALDEGRAVE.

PRINCESS AUGUSTA. Troops.

PRINCESS SOPHIA. More troops.

PRINCESS MARY. Well, thank goodness for the cold collation.

PRINCESS SOPHIA *nods slightly flirtatiously at* ISAAC *before following her sisters out. A pause. We hear a cry and the roll of the carriage wheels departing. There is another pause.* ISAAC *lifts out a big oilskin sailor's rucksack, opens it and slides out a bolt of silk, as:*

MARY. The King. Isaac, I've just been talking to His Majesty, the King.

ISAAC (*opening up the bolt of silk*). He do be two foot off.

MARY. That's . . . silk.

ISAAC. And despite we've got the King of England thinking as we'm honest folk at honest work, likely there be excise men about who's not so trusting.

MARY. But, Isaac, you can get us lace? And woollen stuffs? And satin?

ISAAC. I can . . .

MARY. Then bind me. As you say, there may be customs men about. Bind me, like Mrs Charles was in the song.

A moment. ISAAC *starts to help* MARY *roll the bolt of silk open, as she takes off her coat, to be wrapped in it.*

ISAAC. You must understand, about our trade. This baint just the digging up of stuff on a dark night. This be an operation, with a ship and crew, and landers, and above all that a Venturer.

MARY. A Venturer?

ISAAC. The gentleman as puts the money up. A deal of money. So the stuff can lie snug here till we'm safe to sell her on.

MARY. And is this your father?

ISAAC. Oh no, the Venturer baint the sort of chap as you do come across glutching down a pint or consorting with free traders. No, you'll likely find him in the front pew of the church, or at the mason's lodge, or in the hall of his grand mansion.

MARY. So do I know him? Does he know my father?

ISAAC. 'Tis the biggest secret as I'll ne'er be told.

MARY *has one end of the unrolled bolt of silk,* ISAAC *the other. She spins herself towards him, wrapping the silk around her. When she's reached him, they inevitably fall into each others' arms. He kisses her passionately, and lifts her above him.*

MARY. Secrets. Our time.

He lets her down.

ISAAC. You know, I be furled up in a world I be wanting to be break free from.

She looks at him.

MARY. So am I.

Scene Seven – 'To the flower of Dorchester'

The North Square Theatre and elsewhere, 17th to 31st August. First of all, ELIZABETH MEECH *enters ringing a handbell. She is followed by everyone involved in rehearsals this evening:* MARY, CATHERINE, WILLIAM, MARY SUSANNAH – *who on the quiet is developing a fondness for* BRINE – HAGLEY, ROBERT *and* JANE, CAROLINE HINGE, CHARLOTTE, JOHN FEAVER, ANN HAZARD, EDITH *and* LUCY. MARY FRAMPTON *is in a paint-splattered smock, with her pallette. New members of the company include* PHYLLIS, MARY *and* HARRIET. OLD LEE *stands watching.* JENNY *stands to the side with* HENRY, *who has a large and ominous accounts book.* ELIZABETH MEECH *reads out the call for this evening:*

ELIZABETH MEECH. Ladies and gentlemen, up, up and let's to it! The Judge Jeffreys scene is rehearsing on the stage. The Roman dancers are in the green room. There is a list of costume fittings with Mrs Manfield on the noticeboard in the prompt corner. Anyone not currently engaged is welcome to assist Miss Frampton with the painting of the Great Fire of 1613. Any questions? No. Excellent. Then, to it!

She strides off. As people disperse to their various duties:

MARY SUSANNAH. William. You know what Henrietta says?

WILLIAM. What?

MARY SUSANNAH (*pushing him towards* MARY). To it!

CATHERINE. Miss Stickland. I need you in the wardrobe.

MARY *follows her to the wardrobe as* WILLIAM *is left there, shrugging at a despairing* MARY SUSANNAH.

HENRY. While you and I, Miss Hodge, discuss whether our finances will permit us to present our play this side of Candlemas.

JENNY. Yes, Mr Lee.

As they depart, focus shifts to the costume fitting.
CATHERINE *is fitting* CHARLOTTE, *with* MARY *holding pins.*

CATHERINE. Stand on the chair, please.

CHARLOTTE *stands on the chair.*

CHARLOTTE. Um . . . is this silk?

CATHERINE. Yes. I am placing panels of silk on most of the dresses.

CHARLOTTE. You have found a way of obtaining silk?

Touching the silk.

French silk?

CATHERINE. Please raise your arms.

She measures from CHARLOTTE's *shoulder to the wrist.*

CHARLOTTE. You know . . . I should love at least one of my children to be christened in lace . . .

CATHERINE, *who is behind* CHARLOTTE, *throws a look to* MARY *who, unseen by* CHARLOTTE, *makes a tiny nod.*

CATHERINE. I'll see what I can do.

CHARLOTTE *gets down, smiles, and goes out.*

Miss Stickland. As you might imagine, I am curious to know . . .

MARY. 'The greatest secret as I'll ne'er be told.'

Focus shifts to The Crown Inn. ISAAC *has arrived to see* OLD GULLIVER, *who is stocktaking with* ELIZABETH HARDY *and* EMMANUEL. *Also present – eating their dinner – are* LOVEY, CASSANDRA, HANNAH *and* FRENCH PETER, *with* BILLY *sweeping up.*

OLD GULLIVER. Now, young Isaac, 'tis grand to see you gracing us with your presence.

CASSANDRA. Hardly see him this past month.

ELIZABETH HARDY. Billy, get young Mr Gulliver a mug of beer.

LOVEY. Bet he only sups the finest brandy nowadays.

ISAAC. In fact, that's what I needs to talk to you about.

OLD GULLIVER. Oh, ar?

ISAAC takes the list of requirements from his pocket and gives it to OLD GULLIVER, who takes it aside to read in the light. BILLY brings ISAAC his mug of beer.

ISAAC. You be all right, Billy?

BILLY. Yes, Mr Gulliver. But I do hear there be recruiting parties in the town . . .

Having read the list, OLD GULLIVER comes to ISAAC.

OLD GULLIVER. Silk. Lace. Brandy. I'll need another parley with my Venturer.

(*To* BILLY.) Billy, I needs you to take a message to a gentleman in Dorchester.

The scene shifts to the clifftops at night. ISAAC goes to join MARY. They whisper.

MARY. Where have you been?

ISAAC. I'm sorry. The run be almost made.

MARY. I have a further list. To be purchased by your mysterious 'Venturer'.

ISAAC. Mary!

MARY. It's not that much. Claret for the masons' dinner, playing cards . . . Oh, and our maid's older sister – her husband broke his back and they have seven mouths to feed . . . and with the price of flour . . .

ISAAC (*kissing her*). Oh, Mary Stickland, you do be the death of me.

The churchyard, early morning. Poor WOMEN *and their* CHILDREN – *including* JANEY – *are rubbing out their washing on the flat tombstones. A funeral march is heard. This then turns into a hymn, led by* OLD GULLIVER, *who drives a horse-drawn hearse through the moss-covered tombstones. All of the* SMUGGLERS, *including* BILLY, *march behind the coffin carrying torches.*

ALL.

    Thou turnest Man, O Lord, to dust
    Of which he first was made;
    And when thou speak'st the word, Return
    'tis instantly obeyed.
    For in thy sight a thousand years
    Are like a day that's past,
    Or like a Watch in Dead of Night,
    Whose hours unminded Waste.

With heads bowed, the MOURNERS *lay the coffin to rest on the ground. Together they begin a prayer, interrupted by a whistle. Immediately, one of them hits the side of the coffin, which collapses to reveal a mass of smuggled goods. The* LANDERS *amongst the party take bottles and packets and hide them about their persons. Seeing the* WOMEN *watching them, a couple of the* SMUGGLERS *take small packages of flour and twists of tea to them, plus biscuits for the* CHILDREN, *to buy their silence. Simultaneously, the wood from the coffin is thrown onto the back of the cart – the black feather is removed from the horse's bridle and* OLD GULLIVER *puts on a farmer's hat and leads the cart away. The funeral party nod and evaporate into the town,* BILLY *running off in the other direction.*

Then, all around the space, we see events in which the contraband is being passed out and put to good use by the citizens of Dorchester. First of all, a grand dinner at The Antelope, served by SUSANNAH *and attended by the* EARL, JOHN TEMPLEMAN, JOHN MANFIELD, ROBERT, NATHANIEL *and* GEORGE.

NATHANIEL. For what in Thy bounty it hath been Thy will to grant to us Thy humble servants, we beseech Thee, may we be thankful, oh Lord, our strength and our redeemer.

A moment of respectful silence, then the EARL raises his glass, and takes a sip. Everyone else raises their glass and takes a sip. Everyone cheers and raps the table. Dance music, as CHARLOTTE approaches her sleeping husband GILES, rings a bell to wake him, and places a bottle of claret in his lap.

CHARLOTTE. My dear.

Then, elsewhere, DANCERS at a Grand Ball dance on to the stage. They include: MARY SUSANNAH, MARY FRAMPTON, LUCY, BRINE and HAGLEY, watched by PHYLLIS, MARY STICKLAND, FANNY, EDITH and LUCIA.

LUCIA. Your daughter Mary certainly looks delightful, Mrs Frampton.

PHYLLIS. As does your niece.

EDITH. With her lovely French lace collar.

FANNY. With her satin gloves.

Then, surprisingly – for those of us who haven't been paying attention – we see BOWER in bed with CAROLINE HINGE.

BOWER. Oh, dear!

CAROLINE HINGE. A cup of tea?

Meanwhile, at the MEECHES, a game of whist is in progress. Just one table: HENRIETTA, ELEANOR, JANE and MARIA.

JANE. And now we are in diamonds?

HENRIETTA (*tight-lipped*). Clubs.

ELEANOR. A shame that Mrs Frampton is not here to see the pretty pictures.

HENRIETTA. Or Miss Feaver.

MARIA (*tight-lipped*). Well, indeed.

Back to the dance.

PHYLLIS (*raising a glass*). To the flower of Dorchester!

The dinner.

NATHANIEL. To His Majesty the King!

ALL. His Majesty!

The Crown Inn.

LOVEY. To our benefactor in this time of national peril!

SMUGGLERS. Bonaparte!

The SMUGGLERS applaud. At the same time, the DINNER GUESTS applaud the toasts. The dance ends and both DANCERS and WATCHERS applaud. So now there is applause all round the space. Suddenly, everything stops and we focus on the wardrobe where ISAAC and MARY are rehearsing.

ISAAC. 'I vowed to ride with you on horseback through a misty morning on the Scottish Highlands. Or walk unshod through the sands of Egypt and the prairies of America. Or else . . .' What's wrong?

MARY. You make me want to fly.

ISAAC. 'Or else . . . '

MARY. Maybe we should fly away together.

ISAAC. Steady, Mary.

MARY. I could be your lander . . . your wife . . . unless I am mistaken.

ISAAC. You be sure of your heart?

MARY. As I have been for six weeks and three days. Ever since I wrote the letter at Miss Meech's.

ISAAC. Do you still have it?

MARY. Yes.

MARY *takes the note from her pocket, and hands it over to* ISAAC *to read.*

I pretended I was writing a novella.

ISAAC. '*On se revoit en secret et on le dira a personne.*' ['We will meet in secret and tell no one'.]

ISAAC *reads the letter. As he does so,* WILLIAM *appears in the doorway. He stops, stays back, hiding in the shadows.*

But I have no home, no fortune to offer . . .

MARY *takes out the purse in which she has been collecting the coins for the contraband.*

MARY. That's over fifteen pounds.

ISAAC. That's not ours. 'Tis for the lace and satin.

MARY. We have but one lifetime. And so? Will you?

Slight pause.

ISAAC. Yes.

ISAAC *puts the letter in the pouch. They embrace.*

WILLIAM. I beg your p-p-pardon, I was looking for Mrs Manfield.

ISAAC *and* MARY *spring apart.* MARY *pockets the pouch.*

MARY. We were going through our lines.

ISAAC. The scene where Mary meets with her former sweet-heart Jack in the tearoom.

WILLIAM. Their secret meeting. Just before the wedding.

MARY. Which Miss Hodge has asked dear Mr Swift to play.

WILLIAM (*fingering the silk on a dress*). Well, what fine costumes Mrs Manfield makes. Quite the p-p-p-perfect . . . disguise.

ISAAC. Perhaps . . . this be enough play-acting for one evening.

He goes out, leaving WILLIAM *and* MARY *together.*

MARY. I should attend to . . .

WILLIAM. In the scene, I don't recall any reference to a baccy p-p-pouch.

Slight pause.

Show it me.

MARY *takes out the pouch.*

MARY. It is Mr Swift's. I was . . . holding it for him.

WILLIAM. Then I will return it.

She hands the pouch over. WILLIAM *takes the opportunity to grasp her hand.*

MARY. William . . .

WILLIAM. Mary, there's a time in every man's life . . .

He pulls her to him, in a bid to kiss her.

MARY. Mr Stickland . . .

She pulls herself away and runs out. WILLIAM, *alone, opens the pouch, notes the gold coins inside, takes out the letter and reads it. In the main area, various people, including* ANN HAZARD, LUCY, JANE, CHARLOTTE, PHYLLIS *and* HARRIET, *are reading scripts, practising dance steps, or – in the case of* MARY SUSANNAH *and* BRINE – *canoodling.* MARY *is looking for* ISAAC.

Mr Swift! Have you seen Mr Swift? I have to warn him . . .

Enter BOWER.

BOWER. Where is Miss Hodge?

JANE. She is rehearsing . . .

BOWER. It is the King.

ELIZABETH MEECH. The King?

LUCY runs out to get JENNY, *as* MARY *'borrows' a shawl and puts it over her head.*

CATHERINE (*tidying*). Uh, should we not . . .

BOWER. Apparently he is wont to act on impulse and –

Enter GARTH *and* FITZROY.

GARTH. His Majesty!

FITZROY. Make way for His Majesty the King!

GARTH. Look sharp!

BOWER. – he is inordinately fond of theatre.

Enter KING GEORGE, QUEEN CHARLOTTE, *the* PRINCESSES AUGUSTA, MARY *and* SOPHIA, ELIZA-BETH WALDEGRAVE *and* CAROLINE WALDEGRAVE.

KING GEORGE. This is the play?

JENNY and HENRY *rush in, followed by* CAROLINE HINGE, ROBERT, JOHN FEAVER *and* EDITH, *and* MARY FRAMPTON *and* HAGLEY, *suspiciously bespattered with paint. Also* ISAAC, *who, like* MARY, *moves to the back so* KING GEORGE *won't see him. Finally,* OLD LEE.

QUEEN CHARLOTTE. *Wer ist hier verantwortlich?* [Who's in charge here?]

KING GEORGE. Yes, yes. Where's Mr Lee?

OLD LEE (*flings himself dramatically to the floor in front of* KING GEORGE). Your Majesty, I am Lee.

KING GEORGE. Thank you for your letter.

OLD LEE. I am overwelmed to welcome you to my humble playhouse . . .

HENRY. Your letter?

KING GEORGE. A new play, what what? Will you play it for us tonight?

The PRINCESSES' *eyes roll.*

HENRY. Sir, our play is not yet entirely ready for performance.

KING GEORGE. Not ready? This is a dreadful disappointment.

JENNY (*on impulse*). It will be ready in a week.

HENRY (*whispering*). Miss Hodge!

JENNY. And of course we would be overwhelmed if you . . .

KING GEORGE. A week's time! Capital! Tonight we will dine with . . .

ELIZABETH WALDEGRAVE. The Earl of Dorchester.

CAROLINE WALDEGRAVE. At Came.

QUEEN CHARLOTTE. *Was ist hier los?* [What is going on?]

KING GEORGE (*continuing*). And next week we will return and see the play! So, to it, what what? Splendid! Good luck to one and all!

He turns and goes.

PRINCESS AUGUSTA. Next week we will return to Dorchester to see a play, Mama.

QUEEN CHARLOTTE *flounces out after her husband.*

PRINCESS SOPHIA. Well, at least we'll only have to see it once.

The rest of the ROYAL PARTY *goes out.*

BOWER. Well, Miss Hodge.

ROBERT. The enterprise that the town rejected . . .

OLD LEE. . . . . the Crown approves.

JOHN FEAVER. Let us pray we don't all end up in the Tower.

JENNY. Well, as you say. Now, as we are all gathered, shall we rehearse the song at the end of the first act?

ELIZABETH MEECH. Everybody to your places!

Everyone gets in place for the big song that ends the first act of the play.

HENRY (*to* JENNY). Ready in a *week*? Paid for by . . . ?

JENNY taps the side of her nose, to indicate she has a plan. HENRY strides off. JENNY turns to CATHERINE.

JENNY. I know what's going on. Two pounds in every ten goes to the play.

She goes off, as WILLIAM enters, goes to ISAAC and hands him his pouch.

WILLIAM. Yours, I believe, sir.

A moment. Then:

ELIZABETH MEECH. Everyone ready!

HENRY. One, two, three!

The actors in JENNY'S COMPANY start to sing David Garrick's great patriotic song 'Heart of Oak' , as the Act One closer of their play. The song then moves outwards, from the ACTORS to everyone else, grouped in their classes as GENTRY, SOLDIERY, SMUGGLERS and the POOR. The song swells to a rousing – if ironic – climax.

JENNY'S COMPANY.
 Come, cheer up, my lads, 'tis to glory we steer,
 To add something more to this wonderful year.
 To honour we call you, as free men not slaves,
 For who are so free as the sons of the waves?

 Chorus
 Heart of oak are our ships,
 Jolly tars are our men:
 We always are ready,
 Steady, boys, steady!
 We'll fight and we'll conquer again and again!

SOLDIERS.
>We ne'er see our foes but we wish them to stay.

SMUGGLERS.
>They never see us but they wish us away.

SOLDIERS.
>If they run, why we follow, on sea and on shore.

SMUGGLERS.
>And if they don't catch us, what can we do more?

JENNY'S COMPANY. (*Chorus*)

GENTRY.
>We'll still make them fear and we'll still make them flee

POOR.
>A nation united, contented and free.

JENNY'S COMPANY.
>Then cheer up, brave lads, with one heart let us sing:

EVERYONE ELSE.
>For our soldiers, our sailors, our people, our King!

ALL.
>Heart of oak are our ships,
>Jolly tars are our men:
>We always are ready,
>Steady, boys, steady!
>We'll fight and we'll conquer again and again!

End of Act One.

Interval

*During the interval, the audience becomes gradually aware
that everything on sale from costumed* SALESPEOPLE –
*drinks, snacks, merchandise – is contraband. In addition,
selected members of the audience are approached and asked to
'look after' items. At the end of the Interval,* EXCISE MEN
raid the refreshments and merchandise stalls, dragging the
SALESPEOPLE *away, to reappear at the end of the first scene
of the second act. They also arrest costumed* CITIZENS *who
have received contraband items to 'look after'. None of the
real audience with contraband will be arrested, but they don't
know that.*

ACT TWO

Scene One – 'His heart is dark with scheming'

Pushed in his wheelchair by BENJAMIN, *the* EARL *careers furiously across the stage, watched by the* CHORUS.

EARL. The play? Can this be true? Is this the entertainment which that woman brought up at the meeting? At a time of – were it possible – even greater hazard for our nation and its people, the King himself returns to see a *play*?

He screeches to a halt. The CHORUS *sings a version of the traditional folk ballad 'Blow the Candles Out'. As they do so, groups of* CITIZENS *appear.*

CHORUS.
    The dusk is fast descending
    The August days are gone
    The fruit be ripe to bursting
    The harvest is to come
    Across the fields and meadows
    They whisper all about
    'What's creeping through the darkness
    To blow the candles out?'

    JOHN TEMPLEMAN *and* JOHN MANFIELD *have joined* BENJAMIN *and the* EARL.

    A time of fear and peril
    A time of disarray

JOHN TEMPLEMAN.
    Should we be making merry?

EARL.
    The king attend a *play*?

CHORUS.
> The gentry of the county
> They splutter and they shout.

JOHN MANFIELD.
> The nation is in peril!

CHORUS.
> Don't blow the candle out.

The CHORUS *move on to* MARIA, ELEANOR *and* FANNY.

> Great ladies mourn the passing
> Of innocence and grace

MARIA.
> To everything a season,

ELEANOR.
> To everything its place.

CHORUS.
> Against the winds of winter

FANNY.
> Cast neither cloth nor clout

CHORUS.
> They huddle at their fireside
> Don't blow their candle out.

The CHORUS *moves on to* KEILMANREGGE, USLAU, HENRIETTA *and* ANN HAZARD.

> The soldiers wait for Boney
> Their sweethearts stay in vain.

HENRIETTA.
> Will they be gone forever?

ANN HAZARD.
> Will they come back again?

KEILMANREGGE *and* USLAU.
> By the King we are commanded
> His enemies to rout.

CHORUS.
> So, pray for true love's waiting
> Don't blow your candles out.

The CHORUS *moves on to* MARY STICKLAND *and her daughter* MARY.

> A mother spies her daughter

MARY STICKLAND.
> A-sleeping in her bed.

CHORUS.
> She dreams of when her darling
> A gentleman shall wed.
> The daughter is determined

MARY.
> Her mother's dream to flout.

CHORUS.
> Her childhood bed abandoned.
> So blow the candle out.

Music continues. Dressed in a fine new red uniform, pissed as a newt, BILLY *stumbles through the* AUDIENCE *and among the groups on stage, begging food, chased by two* RECRUITING SERGEANTS *and* HENRY BUSH.

FIRST SERGEANT. There he is!

BILLY. Excuse me, pray . . .

SECOND SERGEANT. After him!

BILLY. Fair ladies, please. A soldier of the king, might you not spare a penny?

FIRST SERGEANT. Stop that man!

BILLY. Fair madam, I've not took a bite since yesterday . . .

The SERGEANTS *leap on* BILLY *and pinion him. The groups melt away, leaving only* MARY *behind.*

FIRST SERGEANT. You're William Lawrence?

BILLY. Aye. And a soldier of / King George!

FIRST SERGEANT. And this morning you volunteers for the 15th Dragoons.

BILLY. And it's the proudest day / of my –

FIRST SERGEANT. And we gives you this here uniform.

SECOND SERGEANT. And a shilling.

FIRST SERGEANT. Which you've obviously spent.

SECOND SERGEANT. Know as how you're under aged.

FIRST SERGEANT. And apprenticed to this gentleman.

SECOND SERGEANT. For which you should be thrown in jail and whipped from here to Weymouth.

BILLY. Please, all I want to do / is serve –

HENRY BUSH. I'll take him back. You said a shilling?

FIRST SERGEANT. And a guinea for the uniform.

HENRY BUSH *hands it over.*

HENRY BUSH. I do promise his father and his mother. But you tries a lark like this again . . .

HENRY BUSH *drags* BILLY *away. The* SERGEANTS *leave. Back to the song, with* MARY, ISAAC, WILLIAM *and* HENRIETTA.

CHORUS.
    The town it sleeps uneasy:

MARY.
    The daughter, will she go?

ISAAC.
    The lover dreams of leaving

MARY.
>A world she longs to know.

CHORUS.
>A man stands in a window

HENRIETTA (*speaking*). William?

CHORUS.
>Full of questioning and doubt . . .

WILLIAM (*speaking*). She loves another.

HENRIETTA. So?

WILLIAM. I will p-p-prevail against him.

CHORUS.
>His heart is dark with scheming
>To blow their candle out.

Above, the CONTRABAND-SELLERS *arrested in the interval, including* HANNAH, *are tied to whipping posts and are being beaten. Below,* DIGNATORIES *and* CITIZENS *of the town – including* JOHN TEMPLEMAN, GILES, GEORGE, MARIA, NATHANIEL *and* ROBERT – *stand watching, and drawing a sober lesson.*

JOHN TEMPLEMAN. Of course, it's all too easy to set our selfish appetites above the greater good.

GEORGE. In fact, I find the pleasures of tobacco much exaggerated.

GILES. It is certainly vital that everyone refrains from conspicuous display. As an example to . . .

EARL. The lower orders.

MARIA. Of course, our old bent playing cards have the charm of age and history.

ROBERT. It's clear we're all agreed on the need for vigilance . . .

NATHANIEL. . . . . against the enemy within.

NATHANIEL *glances at his fobwatch as he and the others* *hurry away. The* YOUNG WOMAN *is there, looking up at* *the* CONTRABAND-SELLERS, *as the scene changes* *around her.*

Scene Two – 'What can darling Mr Swift have done?'

Wednesday 5th September. A rehearsal at the theatre. Just *before rehearsals start.* ISAAC *and* HAGLEY *are setting out* *chairs for a trial scene.* BOWER *is marching up and down* *mouthing lines.* CAROLINE HINGE *watches him indulgently.* MARY *and* HARRIET *are also studying lines.* CHARLOTTE *has the unopened package containing her smuggled lace to* *return to* CATHERINE, *who enters carrying costumes. Enter* ROBERT *and* JANE, *with* JOHN FEAVER. *Seeing her father,* MARY SUSANNAH *breaks away from her intimate conversa-* *tion with* BRINE. CHARLOTTE *catches up with* CATHERINE.

CHARLOTTE (*gesturing with the lace package*). Mrs Man-field, I have determined that despite your generosity, my new child should be christened in plain cotton after all. In the interests . . .

CATHERINE *shushes her, takes the package, and goes out,* *as* ELIZABETH MEECH, JENNY *and* HENRY *come in.*

ELIZABETH MEECH. Good evening, everyone. May we have all parties for the trial scene . . .

HENRY. In the places we agreed on Monday.

JENNY. Major Brine, the apothecary is in the witness box.

Everyone goes to their places.

ELIZABETH MEECH (*to* WILLIAM). Mr Stickland, you are not needed for this scene. You are already poisoned.

WILLIAM. Hence I feel comp-p-p-pelled to witness it.

HENRY (*passing the script to* WILLIAM). Perhaps Mr Stickland could be the prompter.

BRINE. Yes, in fact, Miss Hodge, I fear I am not quite yet in
  full command . . . or indeed that I will be by Saturday . . .

JENNY. Oh, come on, Major Brine. He is but the King of
  England.

MARY SUSANNAH. You will be a marvel to behold.

ELIZABETH MEECH. Now, are we ready? Mr Stickland,
  please, the prosecuting counsel.

ROBERT. Oh yes. 'Mr Wolmington, when did you learn of Mrs
  Channing's visit to your shop?'

BRINE (*playing it wizened and bent and ingratiating*). 'I learnt
  of it from my maid, Amy.'

  JENNY *is looking bemused if not alarmed at* BRINE*'s per-*
  formance. During this, WILLIAM*'s mind is not entirely on*
  the prompting; he glances occasionally at his fobwatch.

ROBERT. 'And what did she report?'

BRINE. 'That Mrs Channing had come in at four o'clock and
  bought some mercury.'

ROBERT. 'And then when you heard that Mr Channing had in
  fact died, after eating boiled rice-milk the morning
  following . . . '

BRINE (*his body increasingly wracked and his performance*
  increasing in intensity). 'I went round and confronted her
  and accused her of . . . of . . . '

WILLIAM (*prompts*). – 'Of p-p-poisoning her husband.'

BRINE. 'Of poisoning her husband. On account of his, um,
  being . . . '

WILLIAM. – 'A dull stick.'

BRINE. Yes, 'a dull stick' and, um, is it 'forced upon her'?

WILLIAM. – 'P-p-pressed up-p-pon . . . '

MARY (*unable to bear it*). 'Pressed upon her . . . '

BRINE. 'By her parents, and . . . '

WILLIAM. – 'Against her will.'

BRINE. 'And she fell on her knees and wept and entreated me for Christ Jesus' sake that I would not say anything of it. Which request – '

JENNY (*interrupting*). Major Brine, can I ask, why you are playing Mr Wolmington as if he was a wizened cripple of great age and consumptive disposition?

BRINE. It was my understanding that in the drama, all apothecaries were wizened cripples of consumptive disposition.

HENRY (*whispers to* JENNY). Romeo and Juliet.

JENNY. Well, yes, Major Brine, that is the general rule. But . . .

BRINE. And I must say, I have been working hard to achieve this character in all its aspects.

MARY SUSANNAH. And to great effect.

JENNY. But in this case, perhaps, we might part from the general rule of playing, and present Mr Wolmington as he clearly was, an upright citizen of honour and authority?

BRINE. Oh.

He tries it out that way.

'Which request I rejected naturally and returned immediately home . . . ?'

JENNY. Perfect!

HENRY. Colonel Bower.

BOWER. 'Mrs Channing, do you wish to cross-examine?'

JOHN FEAVER *enters from his 'costume fitting'. He clanks slightly as he moves.*

JOHN FEAVER. Oh, I beg your pardon.

During the following, he goes to ANN HAZARD *and whispers. She goes out for her 'costume fitting'.*

MARY. 'Yes I do. Mr Wolmington, do I strike you as a woman who would weep and beg and plead?'

BRINE. 'Not here in court, Mrs Channing, surely.'

MARY. 'And might there be another explanation for my kneeling down before you?'

BRINE. 'I suppose . . . '

MARY. 'For instance, to tie a shoelace?'

BRINE. 'Well, yes, certainly . . . '

MARY. 'Well, there we are. And moving on – '

EDITH *enters from outside, in an agitation.*

JOHN FEAVER. Edith!

EDITH. Oh, Miss Hodge. I am so sorry. It's the men.

JENNY. What men?

EDITH. They are . . . I am so thrown about . . .

Enter NATHANIEL *and* MARY STICKLAND, *with* HENRIETTA.

ELIZABETH MEECH. Mrs Feaver, you interrupt / a scene.

NATHANIEL. Miss Hodge. You may care to know that we have just been stopped by men in uniform.

HENRIETTA. Looking for 'the place where they are practising the play'.

JENNY. What men?

Enter PHYLLIS *and* MARY FRAMPTON *from painting.*

MARY STICKLAND. The excise men.

CHARLOTTE. The 'excise men'?

ELIZABETH MEECH. What on earth . . . ?

MARY FRAMPTON. What's happening?

Enter three EXCISE MEN.

FIRST EXCISE MAN. In the name of King George, I must ask that everyone stand fast.

BOWER. May I ask upon what business you're addressed?

SECOND EXCISE MAN. Upon the business of His Majesty. In pursuit of contraband.

JOHN FEAVER *clanks. The* EXCISE MEN *look round –* JOHN FEAVER *and everyone near him look round themselves to see where the noise comes from. As they do so,* CHARLOTTE *delicately hides her package.*

ROBERT. Contraband?

NATHANIEL. Why on earth would you pursue that business here?

SECOND EXCISE MAN. And who might you be?

ROBERT. Nathaniel and Robert Stickland.

JANE. Both former Mayors of Dorchester.

FIRST EXCISE MAN. We're here upon receipt of information furnished to us . . .

WILLIAM *looks concerned.*

SECOND EXCISE MAN. . . . by a patriotic citizen.

ANN HAZARD *comes in, carrying a package. She sees* CHARLOTTE *before she picks up the situation.*

ANN HAZARD. Ah, Mrs Meech. Mrs Manfield says –

ANN HAZARD *now picks up the situation. She drops the package which bursts. It is full of flour. There is a pause. The* SECOND *and* THIRD EXCISE MEN *walk over towards her.*

Um, I . . .

ELIZABETH MEECH. Gentlemen. You said you had come here on the basis of a piece of information. I am sure we'd all welcome knowing what it is.

FIRST EXCISE MAN. Then might you point out Mr Swift?

Pause.

CAROLINE HINGE. Not Mr Swift.

CHARLOTTE. There must be some mistake.

THIRD EXCISE MAN. In which case . . .

ISAAC *comes forward*.

ISAAC. I be Mr Swift.

FIRST EXCISE MAN. Well, well.

MARY SUSANNAH. But . . .

PHYLLIS. What can darling Mr Swift have done?

FIRST EXCISE MAN. And maybe you'd be kind enough to turn out your pockets.

ELIZABETH MEECH. Surely, this isn't necessary . . .

Realising he has no choice, ISAAC *turns his pockets out. The contents include* MARY*'s letter and the money pouch.*

SECOND EXCISE MAN (*picking up the pouch*). And what might this be?

ISAAC. It be my – money.

The SECOND EXCISE MAN *opens the pouch and pours the gold coins on the table*.

THIRD EXCISE MAN. And may we ask how you might find yourself in possession of fifteen gold sovereigns?

SECOND EXCISE MAN. That's – legally.

ELIZABETH MEECH. But surely . . . there must be an explanation.

FIRST EXCISE MAN (*turning and looking round at the* COMPANY). Oh, I'm sure.

ISAAC is trying to take the letter back.

SECOND EXCISE MAN. A pouch or two o' baccy.

FIRST EXCISE MAN. An Italian bonnet.

SECOND EXCISE MAN. Or a cask of brandy.

THIRD EXCISE MAN (*to* ISAAC). Eh, what's that?

ISAAC. It be just . . . a letter.

SECOND EXCISE MAN. Hand it over.

ISAAC. Be private.

FIRST EXCISE MAN. Even so.

He takes the letter, looks at it, is mystified, hands it to the SECOND EXCISE MAN.

SECOND EXCISE MAN. It's in French.

Frisson.

HENRY. Surely it is not a crime –

FIRST EXCISE MAN. So. This is a cultivated company. Who speaks French?

MARY is about to leap in, in the hope that she might mistranslate the letter, but HENRIETTA gets there first.

HENRIETTA. Oh, I speak French.

FIRST EXCISE MAN. Then what does this mean?

He reads, in French, haltingly and with a terrible accent.

'*Depuis notre premiere recontre nous sommes engages dans une cause commune.*' ['Since our first exchange – we are pledged – to a common cause.']

HENRIETTA (*takes the letter*). – 'Since our first exchange, we are pledged to a common cause . . . '

She continues reading.

'*Nous nous recontrerons en secret . . .* ' 'We will meet in secret and tell no one of our intercourse.' '*A partir de maintenant . . .* ' 'From now on, you and I are one.'

FIRST EXCISE MAN. I don't think we need any more, do you?

SECOND EXCISE MAN. 'We will meet in secret.'

THIRD EXCISE MAN. 'Our common cause.'

SECOND EXCISE MAN. 'Our first exchange.'

FIRST EXCISE MAN. Fifteen gold sovereigns.

MARY (*blurts out*). But . . . but . . . the money was . . .

EVERYBODY *looks round desperately at* MARY *to shut her up.*

CATHERINE (*whispering*). Mary, hold your tongue.

MARY *is silenced.*

FIRST EXCISE MAN. I'm sorry, ladies. This must be something of a shock.

(*To* ISAAC, *who is looking desperately at* MARY.) Now, sir, I am presuming Swift is not your real name.

ISAAC. No.

FIRST EXCISE MAN. And what is . . . ?

ISAAC. Isaac Gulliver.

Shock. Various people whisper, 'White wigs.'

THIRD EXCISE MAN. That explains it.

FIRST EXCISE MAN. Isaac Gulliver, we are arresting you for treason against your Liege Lord and Majesty, King George the Third. You will be taken to His Majesty's prison here in Dorchester, then to the magistrate for committal.

SECOND EXCISE MAN. On your way.

As they lead him away, ISAAC *turns back to look desperately at* MARY. MARY *turns to the others.*

MARY. But, Father . . . Uncle . . .

ROBERT. Mary. This is dreadful news, of course.

HENRY. We'd all put so much faith in him.

THIRD EXCISE MAN. Let's go.

Just as they approach the door, there is a sudden sound of trumpeting and drumming.

FIRST EXCISE MAN. What's this?

USLAU *and* KIELMANREGGE *come in, playing instruments in a kind of chaotic fanfare.*

USLAU. Ve are, you zee, returned!

KIELMANREGGE. Ve are two actors more!

USLAU *and* KIELMANREGGE. Hurrah!

They pick up that there's something going on.

USLAU. What's this?

THIRD EXCISE MAN. Smuggling. Spying.

SECOND EXCISE MAN. Treason.

FIRST EXCISE MAN. Good evening, gentlemen.

The EXCISE MEN *take* ISAAC *out.*

KIELMANREGGE. Ve are not velcome?

JENNY. You are more than welcome, gentlemen.

MARY *is distraught.*

MARY STICKLAND. Are you quite well, dear?

MARY *nods.* NATHANIEL *takes out his fobwatch and waves it at* MARY.

NATHANIEL. Quite a shock for all of us. We will see you back at home in time for supper?

HENRY. Four days to go. Back to the trial!

CHARLOTTE. But what about . . .

PHYLLIS. . . . dear Mr Swift?

HENRIETTA (*to* MARY). I'm sure in time you'll see it as a blessed escape.

> MARY, *realising what* HENRIETTA *means, throws a black look at* WILLIAM. *He goes quickly with* HENRIETTA, *following* MARY *and* NATHANIEL. *As the* COMPANY *reassembles,* ELIZABETH MEECH *goes to* MARY.

ELIZABETH MEECH. Mary.

MARY. Please . . .

ELIZABETH MEECH. Am I right in thinking . . . ?

> MARY *looks at her, not sure whether to trust her. Then it all tumbles out.*

MARY. Oh, Miss Meech . . . what I have I done to him, to us, the town . . . There is a man they call the Venturer . . .

ELIZABETH MEECH. Mary. Go home. Tomorrow, tell your mother we are to meet for morning tea and cake.

MARY. Forgive me, but I won't be in the mood to visit . . .

HENRY (*calling*). Miss Stickland!

ELIZABETH MEECH. You will tell me everything.

Scene Three – 'If it's good enough for me and mine'

Thursday 6th September – the next day. Dorchester Prison. Through the darkness we hear a moan, which grows into a scream, which turns into a clanking of chains against bars. As the lights come up, just a little, we see we are in the main workroom in the prison. Along the back wall are a series of individual cells, each with a PRISONER inside. ISAAC sits in one

of these cells. In front of the cages is a long table, on which
WOMEN PRISONERS *sit and sew basic hats.* PRISON
GUARDS *look on. Everyone ignores the screaming and
moaning, which comes from a* WOMAN *locked in one of the
cells. A pipe drips relentlessly.* MARTHA SIMPKINS,
PHOEBE CRUST *and* HANNAH *are at the table making hats,
along with* IDA, MOLLY, GERT, FLOSS, JESS, SARAH,
ADA *and* NELL. ROSE SIBLEY *is sweeping up the remnants
of material from the hats. The children* TILLY, AMY WORM
and SUZANNE WORM *are cutting out patterns.* JANEY, *the
heckler from Maumbury Rings, is measuring them out. They
sing the traditional 'Gaol Song':*

PRISONERS.
> Step in my lass I know your face
> 'Tis nothing in your favour.
> A little time I'll give to you,
> Six months unto hard labour.

ALL.
> *Chorus*
> To my hip fol the day, hip fol the day
> To my hip fol the day fol the di-ge-o.

MARTHA. Hurry up. We be ten hats behind.

JANEY. My fingers do snap off we go any faster.

TILLY. We can't go any faster.

PRISONERS.
> At half past six the bell doth ring
> Unto the chapel we must swing.
> On our bended knees must fall.
> Lord have mercy on us all.

ALL. (*Chorus*)

PHOEBE (*to* ROSE). And you be naught but a hindrance.

HANNAH. Fetch us some tea!

ROSE. Please, I be servant to Mrs Andrews, not / to you.

AMY. I'll help you, Rose.

> MARTHA *stands to beat* ROSE *when a huge door is unlocked. A shaft of light floods into the room.*

SUZANNE. Look out!

JANEY. Everybody!

PHOEBE. Back to work!

> *Down the flight of stairs comes the terrifying* MRS ANDREWS. *Even the* GUARDS *stand a little straighter. She is pregnant and carries a small* CHILD.

MRS ANDREWS.
> At eight o'clock the turnkey comes
> With a bunch of keys all in her hand;
> And if one word they chance to say
> To bread and water all next day.

ALL. (*Chorus*)

MRS ANDREWS. Get up. All of you, to your feet. Gulliver! You do have a visitor!

ADA. Fancy ladies.

IDA. Pretty long hair.

MOLLY (*snipping her scissors in the air*). Let 'em sit by me.

> *All of the* PRISONERS *stand, as* MRS ANDREWS *ushers* ELIZABETH MEECH *and* MARY *in.*

PRISONERS.
> At ten o'clock the doctor was round
> With pen and paper in his hand,
> And if we say we are not ill
> So all next day to the treading mill.

ALL. (*Chorus*)

MRS ANDREWS (*to her* GUESTS). Of course, we do aim to get lamps direct. And mebbe fires in the winter. But I do cook up like a hearty broth and what do I always say, ladies, if it's good enough for me and mine . . .

PRISONERS. . . . it's good enough for us.

> ELIZABETH MEECH *and* MARY *are horrified by their surroundings.* MARY *keeps very close to* ELIZABETH MEECH.

JESS. Look at 'em.

SARAH. Want to help us?

MOLLY. Want to make a pretty hat?

GERT. Could match your scarf.

FLOSS (*taking* ELIZABETH MEECH's *scarf*). Such a little neck.

NELL. Look like it could break . . .

> *Other* PRISONERS *clank their mugs on the table and hiss.* HANNAH *recognises* MARY, *who puts a finger to her lips.*

MARTHA. Go on, dare you, like.

PHOEBE. To come and sit with us.

> *More laughter and stamping of feet.*

MRS ANDREWS. Enough, ladies. Let me escort you both to Mr Gulliver.

> FLOSS *drops the scarf and walks away.*

ELIZABETH MEECH. I have no need to see him.

MRS ANDREWS. Then our Rose will make you tea. Ladies, I believe it's dinner time.

> *As* MRS ANDREWS *takes* MARY *to* ISAAC, ROSE, *the* CHILD *and the* PRISONERS *go out.*

PRISONERS.
> At twelve o'clock our beef comes in
> Sometimes fat and sometimes lean
> But a devil of a word we must not say
> Or to bread and water all next day.

TILLY/SUZANNE/AMY. (*Chorus*)

MRS ANDREWS. Now, Mr Gulliver, your visitor do bring you a fine basket. What do you say to that?

ISAAC *stares at the floor, refusing to have eye contact with* MARY.

Speak your thanks, boy.

ISAAC. My thanks.

MRS ANDREWS. Five minutes.

MRS ANDREWS *goes back to the main area. Once she is gone,* MARY *runs to* ISAAC *and tries to hug him. He doesn't respond. She stands back. They stare at each other.*

MARY. Isaac . . . I'm sorry.

ISAAC *turns away.*

Isaac, please, talk to me.

Pause.

ISAAC. I never sleeps a wink last night. 'How could she stand by and say nothing?'

MARY. Isaac, I'm here!

ISAAC. Mary Stickland. Who wants to be my lander.

MARY. Isaac, I couldn't . . .

ISAAC. You got any notion what 'tis to be a smuggler? To be cheated, mebbe, or maimed, or even killed a-fetching the goods home? Oh, ay, I knows full well there be those in the gang are set to spying. But not me. That's why I do set my heart on getting out of this. All I wanted, just enough to get me by. And then you comes along. And noggerhead as I be, I be taken in by your perty looks. And for a while I reckon I could be like you. 'And now, this!'

Pause.

MARY. But – I love you.

ISAAC. Grow up, and fast, Miss Stickland.

MARY. What can I do?

ISAAC. Tell them about us, say it was you do write the letter.

MARY. They will ask about the money.

ISAAC. Then you must say the truth.

MARY. But my family. Your Venturer.

ISAAC. I do be arraigned at the Mayor's house tomorrow.

MARY. 'Concealment is better than injury.'

ISAAC. They – will – hang – me.

He turns away. MARY, *trapped in the cell until* MRS
ANDREWS *returns, stands, unable to do or say anything.*
ROSE *enters, approaching* ELIZABETH MEECH *with a
ludicrously elaborate tea set on a tray.*

ROSE. Mrs Andrews says she'm sorry, she's seeing to a
prisoner.

The WOMAN *in the cell groans loudly.*

ELIZABETH MEECH (*nodding*). Are you their child?

ROSE (*pouring*). No, miss. Mother be a prisoner here.

Pause.

ELIZABETH MEECH. What did your mother do before . . .
this?

ROSE. She be in service, miss.

Pause.

ELIZABETH MEECH. And, where is she?

ROSE (*nodding to the* GROANING WOMAN). That be her,
miss.

Pause.

ELIZABETH MEECH. Do you have any toys here?

ROSE. No time for play. I do like singing, though.

ELIZABETH MEECH. Will you sing for me?

> ROSE *sings. At the same time,* MRS ANDREWS *goes to* ISAAC's *cell and gestures* MARY *to come out.* ISAAC *doesn't turn to* MARY.

ROSE.
> *Le point du jour des nos borquets*
> *rend toutay lur par ury*
> *Floree plus belle a sun retour*
> *L'oiseau reprenday ducks chant d'amour*
> *Toute celebray dans la nature*
> *Le point du jour.*

> *Recognising the song,* ELIZABETH MEECH *looks at* ROSE *in horror.*

ELIZABETH MEECH. How do you know that song?

ROSE. Mama do sing it to me. The lady she'm working for, she do sing it sometimes. Comical words though. Reckon it's a lover song.

ELIZABETH MEECH. Yes, it is.

> ELIZABETH MEECH *glances to make sure the* PRIS- ONERS *aren't watching. She picks up her red silk scarf, quickly ties it into the shape of a doll and gives it to the girl.*

Here, until I can send you something better.

> MRS ANDREWS *brings* MARY *to* ELIZABETH MEECH. MARY *looks ashen and distraught.*

MRS ANDREWS. Ah, tea. Miss, do you want a cup?

MARY (*looking at* ELIZABETH MEECH *watching* ROSE). No, I think I'd like to . . .

> ELIZABETH MEECH *gestures to* MRS ANDREWS *to withdraw, which she does.*

Oh, Miss Meech . . .

> *She runs weeping into* ELIZABETH MEECH's *arms.*

ELIZABETH MEECH. There, there. Let us leave this awful place. And we'll determine what's to do.

She leads MARY *towards the great door, followed by* MRS ANDREWS. ROSE *rocks the doll and sings it the French lullaby.*

Scene Four – 'I have a friend who knows'

The Crown Inn. OLD GULLIVER, EMMANUEL, ELIZA-BETH HARDY, LOVEY, CASSANDRA, FRENCH PETER, LIZZIE, KATIE *and* BESSIE *are sitting at inn tables at one side of the room, with* ELIZABETH MEECH, CATHERINE *and* MARY *on the other. They have just made a proposal.*

LOVEY. You must be chaffing us.

MARY. No. Please –

ELIZABETH MEECH (*interrupts, to the* SMUGGLERS). Why not?

ELIZABETH HARDY. Well, first, as how he's so damn silly as to let himself get caught.

CASSANDRA. And leaving us a-owing five nights' pay to all the landers . . .

FRENCH PETER. And the captain, more's the point.

ELIZABETH MEECH. But, think of the poor boy . . .

OLD GULLIVER. And that's not to mention how he's clapped up tight in Dorchester Jail.

ELIZABETH MEECH. But, Mr Gulliver, your son will be taken from the prison to the Mayor's house in High West Street for committal.

EMMANUEL. Under armed guard, no doubt.

MARY. And, Miss Warne, are you not the finest female shot in all the kingdom?

KATIE. If she's caught with her gun it's death without clergy.

MARY. *If.*

ELIZABETH MEECH. And are not those you will be protecting among the most distinguished and important persons in the county?

ELIZABETH HARDY (*heavily sarcastic*). Oh, well, in that case . . .

CATHERINE. And your customers.

EMMANUEL. But most of all because it's espionage they's took him for –

BESSIE. – and that *is* a hanging matter.

MARY. And maybe . . . it isn't just your customers you'd be protecting.

Pause.

EMMANUEL. What do you mean?

MARY. Isaac spoke of someone who . . . is essential to your current and your future success. Is he called a 'Venturer'?

OLD GULLIVER. What number High West Street?

ELIZABETH MEECH. Number 15.

CATHERINE. Why d'you ask?

OLD GULLIVER. Because there be a tunnel run up High West Street from The White Hart via The King's Arms to the Top o'Town, and as I recollect number 15's on the north side too.

ELIZABETH MEECH. A tunnel?

ELIZABETH HARDY (*mockingly*). So happen there's a party who do know if number 15 has a cellar / and if so –

CATHERINE. Um, actually . . . I could assist with that.

ELIZABETH HARDY. You could?

CATHERINE. I have a . . . friend who knows . . . someone who is a frequent visitor. To . . . the Mayor's house.

The SMUGGLERS *look at each other.*

LIZZIE. Sit you down.

Scene Five – 'A little business overhead'

High West Street, the next day – Friday 7th September. The Manfields' house, number 15, consists of the kitchen on the ground floor – with a trapdoor leading to a cellar below – and the back stairs up to the library on the first floor. There is also much activity in the streets on this fine late-summer afternoon, introduced to us by the CHORUS.

CHORUS. And at three o'clock the next afternoon it was a normal market day in Dorchester.

Immediately, music, an amazing flurry of activity: sheep and cattle being driven down High West Street towards the Shambles, BAKERS *and* BREWERS *with trays of pies and beer plying their trade,* PEDDLARS, ENTERTAINERS, FARMERS *bringing produce,* TOWNSPEOPLE *of many kinds,* CHILDREN *playing hopscotch, watched by the* YOUNG WOMAN. *In the midst of all this, we note many people we know, including* MARY FRAMPTON *and* HARRIET, HENRIETTA *with* ADA GAPE, MARIA, WILLIAM, TOM CHAFFLEY *and* EDWARD, JOHN TEMPLEMAN, GILES, LIZZIE *and* ANN CRAWFORD.

– Amid the flurry of the market, Miss Mary Frampton,

– with her sister Harriet,

– meets two of the remaining members of Miss Meech's whist circle.

HARRIET (*to* HENRIETTA). Why, Miss Meech. Henrietta. What a lovely day.

MARY FRAMPTON. Do you care to join us in our walk?

HENRIETTA. I fear we are on a mission from my mother.

ADA GAPE. Chocolates.

CHORUS. And Miss Stickland's pale-faced distant cousin William . . .

MARY FRAMPTON. Have you seen your cousin Mary? Since . . .

MARIA. Since the unnecessary dramas caused by this unnecessary play.

HENRIETTA. Perhaps she's taken to her bed.

CHORUS. And Reverend Giles Meech, headed to St Peter's, passes John Templeman headed in the opposite direction –

GILES. Alderman.

JOHN TEMPLEMAN. Good afternoon.

CHORUS. And who would notice,

   – on such a bustling afternoon,

   – two ladies, seemingly of the first respectability,

   – glancing idly into the window of Miss Hazard's sweetshop,

   – but in fact noting through the reflection in the glass what was happening at number 15 opposite . . .

LIZZIE. Go to The King's Arms and tell them we are ready for them to go into the tunnel.

ANN CRAWFORD. I be all joppity-joppity. You go and I keeps watch.

CHORUS. . . . where ten minutes earlier, a young smuggling man had been brought for arraignment before the magistrates,

*The town's activity ceases and its people freeze and look at
the house.* ISAAC *is brought into the house by two*
GUARDS, *taken through the kitchen – currently populated
by the* MANFIELDS' COOK *and* MAID *– and up the back
stairs to the library, where* JOHN MANFIELD, JOHN
TEMPLEMAN, NATHANIEL *and* ROBERT *and the first
two* EXCISE MEN *await them.*

FIRST GUARD. – was brought into the house,

MAID. – and up the back stairs

A GUARD *goes up with* ISAAC, *leaving the other two*
GUARDS *in the kitchen with the* MAID *and* COOK.

SECOND GUARD. – to the library.

As ISAAC *is placed in position before the* MAGISTRATES,
the GUARD *standing behind,* CATHERINE *comes into the
kitchen.*

CATHERINE (*to the* GUARDS). Why, gentlemen.

COOK. – said Mrs Manfield,

CATHERINE. On such a hot day, would you like something to
slake your thirst?

As the hearing begins upstairs, the MAID *and* COOK *serve
beer to the* GUARDS. *We move back outside, and the bustle
and swirl recommences.*

CHORUS. While round the corner Mr Edward Fudge
approached the back door of The Antelope,

– to make a request on behalf of his friend, Tom Chaffley.

EDWARD. Such a broiling morning,

TOM CHAFFLEY. – and his spirits so dashed like,

EDWARD. – what with th'arrest of his dear Janey,

TOM CHAFFLEY. – and five children motherless and all.

SUSANNAH. 'A'pence a pint.

TOM CHAFFLEY *and* EDWARD *show their empty pockets.*

CHORUS. But before she slammed the door shut, Mrs Carter noticed

SUSANNAH . – a small cart with a pile of straw,

CHORUS. – and an old man at the reins of what appeared to be

SUSANNAH . – a speedy horse.

TOM CHAFFLEY *and* EDWARD *have gone on to the next pub,* SUSANNAH *stands watching as* BILLY *approaches* OLD GULLIVER *sitting on the cart.*

BILLY. Please, sir. Please, sir . . . Why, Mr Gulliver.

OLD GULLIVER. Where the hell you been?

BILLY. So much do happen since I do see you last.

OLD GULLIVER. Billy, this baint the best o'times . . .

BILLY. I signs up for the 15th Dragoons and I be arrested and I be taken 'fore the magistrate and I be sent back to my master and I 'scapes again and I be off to Bridport and the 40th Dragoons and he's arter me again and I –

OLD GULLIVER. Billy, jump up.

BILLY *jumps into the back of the cart.*

CHORUS. While back at 15 High West Street . . .

Into the kitchen, where the GUARDS *are enjoying their beer with* CATHERINE, *the* COOK *and the* MAID.

FIRST GUARD. A very fine glass you serve here, Mrs Manfield.

SECOND GUARD. You might find us dropping by with desperate felons every day.

CATHERINE. Oh . . . must you?

FIRST GUARD. These smugglers. For all the romancin' 'bout them, you'd not be wanting to come near a hundred miles of 'em.

CATHERINE. No, I'd imagine –

The trapdoor flies open and the SMUGGLERS *come through. The first through is* LOVEY *with her gun cocked, grabbing* CATHERINE *and pointing the gun at her head.* FRENCH PETER *has his gun too, and he grabs the* MAID *and puts a gun to her head.* EMMANUEL *and* CAS-SANDRA *are next up.*

FIRST GUARD. What the devil – ?

LOVEY. Now this be the arrangement for all those who don't want to see this fine lady's head blown off.

FRENCH PETER. Or this little lady's.

LOVEY. They makes nary a peep, the gentlemen do move their chairs like back to back, the ladies they do sit down in a similar configuration.

The GUARDS, *the* MAID *and the* COOK *do as they're told.* LOVEY *nods at* CASSANDRA *and* EMMANUEL, *who go and wind rope round the two pairs and then gag them.*

FRENCH PETER. And the back stairs, they might be this way?

CATHERINE *nods.*

LOVEY. Now if you'll forgive us, we do have a little business overhead.

She leaves CATHERINE *to go upstairs.*

CATHERINE (*feebly*). Help, help!

LOVEY. Once the lady of the house be dealt with, mind.

CASSANDRA *ties* CATHERINE *to a chair.* LOVEY *hands a second pistol to* CASSANDRA.

EMMANUEL. Any trouble, you knows what to do.

FRENCH PETER *leads* LOVEY *and* EMMANUEL *up the back stairs, into:*

JOHN MANFIELD. Therefore we are convinced there is clear evidence of espionage.

NATHANIEL. We are.

JOHN MANFIELD. And I commit you for trial at the upcoming / assizes –

ISAAC. Sir, you might regret that.

ROBERT. What?

FIRST EXCISE MAN. Silence, lad.

ISAAC. On account of summat as I've got to say.

JOHN TEMPLEMAN. Save it for your trial.

ISAAC. Mebbe there's some here as might not welcome that.

NATHANIEL. What do you mean?

ISAAC. There's some here as might not welcome that. Seeing how there be another party in this room who'm caught up in this venture.

ROBERT. What?

> ISAAC *looks to* ROBERT, *as* FRENCH PETER *bursts into the room, followed by* LOVEY *and* EMMANUEL.

FRENCH PETER. Isaac. To me.

> ISAAC *quickly follows* FRENCH PETER *to the window.*

GUARD. Hey –

EMMANUEL. Nobody move.

> FRENCH PETER *whistles through the window.*

JOHN MANFIELD. What's this?

LOVEY. Sit down.

ROBERT. Damned if I'll –

LOVEY (*gun to his head*). Damned if you won't. Which is Manfield?

JOHN MANFIELD. Um, I . . .

NATHANIEL. What in God's name / is this –

LOVEY. 'Cos his missus's down below tied up with a gang of the most desperate ruffians in Europe.

FRENCH PETER (*looking out of the window*). Isaac, go.

ISAAC jumps out of the window and our sight.

LOVEY. Anybody do make a peep in the next ten minutes, Mrs Manfield's singing with the angels.

She heads back out to the stairs, followed by FRENCH PETER and EMMANUEL. As they go back down into the kitchen, in the street, LIZZIE returns to ANN CRAWFORD.

ANN CRAWFORD. Be it all well?

LIZZIE. Far as I knows.

The MANFIELDS' kitchen.

FRENCH PETER. Do go?

CASSANDRA. Do go.

LOVEY. Let's bustle!

They go down the trapdoor. LOVEY is the last, and speaks just before she closes the trap.

With apologies for the . . . discommodation.

The trapdoor falls shut.

Scene Six – 'I fear this is an error'

Meanwhile, the CHORUS describes the dairy cart's thrilling journey from High West Street into the countryside.

CHORUS. Mr Gulliver gees up his steed,

  – and the dairy cart careers up High West Street

  – to the Top o' Town,

– makes a sharp left turn down the Walks,

– scattering the ladies making their perambulations

– (as Miss Frampton immediately notes down in her diary).

– And as the excise men gather pace in their pursuit,

– the cart, with its two secret passengers,

– makes tidy progress towards Weymouth –

– when it comes

– into fierce collision

– with another.

The dairy cart, with the dazed OLD GULLIVER, ISAAC and BILLY thrown from it, lies on its side. A wheel rolls on from the vehicle with which it has been in collision.

BILLY. What . . . what happened?

All three EXCISE MEN enter and rush to ISAAC.

ISAAC. Uh . . .

OLD GULLIVER. Isaac, get up . . .

ISAAC. What?

FIRST EXCISE MAN. All right. One move from you, and you joins the choir invisible.

ISAAC slowly puts out his hands, which the SECOND EXCISE MAN ties.

SECOND EXCISE MAN. And his accomplice.

BILLY. No.

As the FIRST EXCISE MAN is about to tie BILLY's hands, enter KING GEORGE, with GARTH and FITZROY. They are brushing themselves down, following the collision.

KING GEORGE. What's this, what what?

The EXCISE MEN recognise KING GEORGE immediately and fall to their knees. OLD GULLIVER climbs to his knees.

EXCISE MEN. Your Majesty.

KING GEORGE. What's this?

SECOND EXCISE MAN. Please assure us you have sustained
no injury.

KING GEORGE. I'm splendid.

FITZROY. Not a scratch.

FIRST EXCISE MAN. Then, sir, you are witnessing the arrest
of a notorious smuggler and spy . . .

KING GEORGE (*seeing* ISAAC). There must be some mistake.

Pause.

SECOND EXCISE MAN. With respect, sir, I assure you –

Enter the slightly shaken QUEEN CHARLOTTE, *the*
PRINCESSES AUGUSTA, MARY *and* SOPHIA, *and*
ELIZABETH WALDEGRAVE *and* CAROLINE WALDE-
GRAVE.

QUEEN CHARLOTTE. *Manchmal glaube ich dass es besser
wäre zu Fuss zu gehen.* [I sometimes think it would be better
to walk.]

KING GEORGE. I know this gentleman.

PRINCESS MARY. Mama sometimes thinks it would be better
to walk, Papa.

EXCISE MEN. Your Majesty. Your Royal Highnesses.

PRINCESS AUGUSTA. Or stay at home.

CAROLINE WALDEGRAVE. Why, isn't that the . . . irrigation
man?

KING GEORGE. Indeed. I fear there is an error. This man is
not a smuggler or a spy. Release him immediately!

THIRD EXCISE MAN. Sir, we must insist . . .

The SECOND EXCISE MAN *realises which side his bread
is buttered, and releases* ISAAC.

QUEEN CHARLOTTE. *Ist das nicht der Mann, den wir schon vorher getroffen haben?* [And is that not the man we met before?]

PRINCESS MARY. Yes, it's the same man, Mama.

ELIZABETH WALDEGRAVE. And the boy?

BILLY. This worthy publican do transport me on my way to sign up for service in your 40th Dragoons at Bridport.

He proudly points to the ribbons on his hat and salutes.

'Tis allus my dream, Your Majesty . . . to . . .

BILLY*'s overwhelmed.*

PRINCESS AUGUSTA (*whispers to* FITZROY). He can hardly be fourteen . . .

KING GEORGE. Yes, capital. Garth, take this young man and deliver him to his regiment post-haste.

GARTH. It would be . . . my pleasure.

KING GEORGE. Good luck, young man, and may you serve your sovereign for many years to come!

A ripple of applause. GARTH *tosses his head towards* BILLY*, who salutes, turns and marches off.*

That's all settled, what what? Is the carriage yet in a condition for our onward travel?

FITZROY. Yes, sir.

KING GEORGE. Then – to Dorchester!

The PRINCESSES *look at each other morosely, as* KING GEORGE *turns to go. The* EXCISE MEN *smile maliciously at* ISAAC*, who they can and will arrest as soon as* KING GEORGE *has departed. As this happens:*

QUEEN CHARLOTTE. *Und was passert jetzt?* [What is happening now?]

PRINCESS AUGUSTA. We're going to the play, Mama.

PRINCESS SOPHIA. It's a history of Dorchester.

PRINCESS MARY. You'll love it.

This gives ISAAC *an idea.*

ISAAC. Your Majesty. As it happens, I be in the play.

KING GEORGE. What what?

ISAAC. And I fear as, with the time it takes to put the wheel back on our vehicle . . .

PRINCESS SOPHIA. Papa, there's room in our carriage.

OLD GULLIVER. Isaac.

ISAAC. And my father. Who be also . . . in the play.

KING GEORGE. And will ride with me.

FIRST EXCISE MAN. But, sir . . .

KING GEORGE (*to* OLD GULLIVER, *walking him out*). Mr Swift. You must be so proud of your son. And your beauteous daughter-in-law.

OLD GULLIVER. I beg your pardon?

Before ISAAC *goes:*

FIRST EXCISE MAN. Rest assured, we'll be at the play.

SECOND EXCISE MAN. We'll watch your every move.

THIRD EXCISE MAN. And we'll see you afterwards.

ISAAC *goes with the* ROYAL PARTY.

FIRST EXCISE MAN. Eh?

Scene Seven – 'You must let me go'

Backstage at the North Square Theatre, later the same day: at the stage door, in the wardrobe, the male and female dressing rooms, the candle store and the main rehearsal area. Some in costume, mostly not, the COMPANY *enters:* MARY SUSANNAH, CHARLOTTE, EDITH, CAROLINE HINGE, ANN HAZARD, MARY, HARRIET *and* PHYLLIS, ELIZABETH MEECH, JANE, LUCY, WILLIAM *and* GEORGE, *who has joined the company,* JOHN FEAVER, ROBERT, BOWER, USLAU, KIELMANREGGE, BRINE, HAGLEY, OLD LEE, HENRY, MARY *and her mother* MARY STICKLAND, *and* JENNY. *The* COMPANY *sings the warm-up song for the show.*

HENRY (*giving note*). MMMMMMMMMM . . .

ALL. MMMMMMMMM . . .

HENRY. One, two, three four . . .

ALL.
>A – E – I – O – U
>B – B – D – D – T
>Nn Mm Bb Nn Mm Bb
>Bitter butter bitter butter bit
>Better butter better butter bit
>Cla – ri – ty in speech
>Pro – nounce it trip – ping – ly
>Don't forget to breathe!
>And tune your note with me
>Meeeeeeeeeeeeeeeeeeeeeeee
>Now in harmony let us merrily sing
>Soprano, alto, tenor, bass
>God save the King!
>God save the King!
>God save the King!

    Confusion to the French, huzzah!
    And God save the King!

At the end, the COMPANY *applauds itself.* ELIZABETH
MEECH *nudges* LUCY, *who has taken on an important
stage-management role.*

LUCY. Ten minutes! Ten minutes, everyone!

The COMPANY *splits to go to the male and female dressing
rooms,* JENNY *to wardrobe. The* OFFICERS *blow kisses at*
ANN HAZARD *and* MARY SUSANNAH. *Gossip flows.*

CAROLINE HINGE. As I understand it, nobody was harmed.

JANE. You mean, during the outrage at the Mayor's house.

CHARLOTTE. Mrs Manfield, so I hear, behaved heroically.

JANE. Unlike her husband.

MARY FRAMPTON. Who's taken to his bed.

PHYLLIS. And does anyone have news of dear Mr Swift?

MARY, hearing this, turns to move away, bumping into
WILLIAM. *By now the main area is empty.*

WILLIAM. Miss Stickland. Mary!

MARY. I have nothing that I wish to say to you.

WILLIAM. I did what I thought was for the best. For you, for
    me, for everyone.

JENNY comes in from the wardrobe, in ISAAC's *costume,
buttoning up her shirt.*

JENNY. Ah, Mary. Could I have a word?

WILLIAM. I offered you a home.

*MARY STICKLAND comes back in from the dressing room
to find her daughter.*

MARY STICKLAND. Mary, come and let me do your hair.

WILLIAM. I can still give you that.

MARY STICKLAND. What's happening?

MARY. Mama. If I thought that this would be of the slightest
benefit, I would tell this . . . gentleman, that I have never in
my life known a more pampered, selfish, spoilt little boy.

*NATHANIEL enters from the street. He holds a bouquet of
flowers, discreetly.*

NATHANIEL. Ah. Mary.

MARY STICKLAND. Nathaniel?

MARY. He is injured, not by my refusal, but because, for the
first time in his life, someone has said 'no'.

*She turns and goes briskly out towards her dressing room;
MARY STICKLAND shrugs at her husband and follows
quickly.*

WILLIAM (*to* NATHANIEL). I know she's angry *now* . . .

WILLIAM goes off to his dressing room.

NATHANIEL. So that was – in the play?

JENNY. Not entirely. Would that our real lives could be
resolved as easily as those on stage.

Enter ROBERT from the men's dressing room.

ROBERT. Ah, Miss Hodge. I fear we appear to have mislaid
two lawyer's wigs and a bishop's mitre.

JENNY. Well, I will seek them out.

ROBERT (*noticing* NATHANIEL). Brother.

NATHANIEL. Brother.

*JENNY sees FITZROY entering with ISAAC from the
street.*

ROBERT. After the events of this afternoon, I imagine you are
looking forward to a drama of the make-believe variety.

NATHANIEL. Yes, though I fear –

ISAAC. Miss Hodge.

JENNY. Do I see a ghost?

ROBERT. Good God.

FITZROY. Madam. Gentlemen. My name is Fitzroy. This is, I understand, a participant in your performance, whom I have escorted here at His Majesty's express command.

ISAAC. So that I do play my part.

FITZROY *clicks his heels and goes out.*

Yet, mebbe, after what do happen / here this afternoon . . .

JENNY. Yes, of course. The candle store? And I will bring your costume.

ISAAC *goes into the candle store.*

Gentlemen. I trust that you can keep a confidence.

ROBERT. Of course.

JENNY *goes out.*

Nathaniel –

NATHANIEL (*re: the bouquet*). Robert, I wonder, might you give these to my daughter? As I believe is customary.

LUCY (*crossing through and out*). Five minutes! Five minutes, everyone!

ROBERT (*a little bemused*). Of course.

He goes out. NATHANIEL is left alone. He looks at his fob-watch, then goes into the candle store. ISAAC is not surprised to see someone, but he is surprised that it's NATHANIEL.

ISAAC. Mr Stickland.

NATHANIEL. Mr Gulliver. You will forgive me if I speak directly.

ISAAC. Yes?

NATHANIEL. Now you have 'returned', what are your
    intentions?

ISAAC. Well, I do lose the King's protection in two hours.

NATHANIEL. And then you'll flee.

ISAAC. I do have no choice.

NATHANIEL. Never to return.

ISAAC. I fear . . .

NATHANIEL. And never to see Mary's face again.

Pause.

ISAAC. Sir?

NATHANIEL. Mr Gulliver, only her mother can have failed to
    notice your designs upon her.

ISAAC. My 'designs'?

NATHANIEL. You must understand that what was once . . .
    unworthy, is now impossible . . .

ISAAC. Oh, 'tis 'unworthy', / 'tis it?

NATHANIEL. And unless you are prepared to ruin both our
    families –

ISAAC. Mr Stickland, I've nary tuppence to my name.

A moment.

NATHANIEL. I understand.

He takes out a purse and hands it to ISAAC, *who looks
    inside it.*

ISAAC. Not enough.

NATHANIEL. That's all I have about me.

ISAAC. I do need to set myself up in my new life abroad.

NATHANIEL. Well, as I say . . .

ISAAC. Your watch. And you do never see or hear . . .

Slight pause.

NATHANIEL. Why not?

He takes his fobwatch off his waistcoat.

ISAAC. And now you do tell me why you say, 'both our families'.

Slight pause.

NATHANIEL. Why do you think I said it?

ISAAC. I do reckon as it be your brother Robert.

NATHANIEL. Who 'be' my brother?

ISAAC. The Venturer.

Slight pause.

But, 'tis you . . .

In the wardrobe, JENNY is looking at herself, still in ISAAC's costume, in a mirror. She begins to unbutton her shirt, when she sees the YOUNG WOMAN in the reflection.

JENNY. It's you.

YOUNG WOMAN. I wanted to say thank you.

JENNY. 'Thank you'?

YOUNG WOMAN. But you must let me go.

Slight pause.

JENNY. Why?

Back in the candle store. During this, MARY, now costumed, crosses from her dressing room to the warbrobe.

ISAAC. Why?

NATHANIEL. Mr Gulliver. I am not a landowner. I do not possess a fine estate or acreage in Fordington. I have had to bring up a family in the manner they expect by my own efforts.

Hands him the fobwatch.

And I will never see or hear of you again.

ISAAC. I understand.

NATHANIEL. Now, play your part. And I'll play mine.

NATHANIEL *leaves* ISAAC *and goes out, passing* LUCY, *crossing the main area*.

LUCY. Beginners! Miss Hodge and all the chorus for the opening! Beginners, please.

MARY *knocks at the door of the wardrobe*. JENNY *looks to the* YOUNG WOMAN, *who nods*.

JENNY. Come in.

MARY *enters*.

MARY. Oh, I . . . I thought you were with someone.

JENNY *throws a slight glance at the* YOUNG WOMAN, *then back to* MARY.

Miss Hodge, you asked for me?

JENNY. There was something that I wanted you to know.

MARY. Yes?

JENNY. The Earl of Dorchester once asked me why I returned here. And why I strove to mount this play.

MARY. And?

JENNY. Of course, I could have stayed in Paris. But my mother needed me in her last years.

MARY. And the play?

JENNY. Well . . .

JENNY *looks to the* YOUNG WOMAN.

YOUNG WOMAN. Tell her.

JENNY. You know Mary Channing pleaded her belly . . .

MARY. Yes, of course.

JENNY. The child survived.

Pause.

He grew up, married, and had children of his own.

MARY. Yes, I always wondered . . .

JENNY. Six years ago, I found a blue enamel locket made up to mark the marriage of his second son. Here it is.

She shows MARY *the locket round her neck.*

MARY. Where was it?

JENNY. Round my dead mother's neck.

Slight pause.

You are playing my great-grandmother.

Slight pause.

MARY. So, all of this . . . for her?

YOUNG WOMAN. 'Tis true, I was condemned to a dull and tiresome marriage to a man I didn't love.

JENNY. It's true, she was condemned to marriage to a grocer.

YOUNG WOMAN. But I was guilty. What I did was terrible.

JENNY. But . . . she was . . . What she did was . . . terribly misguided. She was just nineteen.

YOUNG WOMAN. And I tried to tear up my life so far and write a new one. A time in which I'd always be dancing, and I'd never have to . . .

JENNY (*directly to the* YOUNG WOMAN). But once we've had that moment, how can we not keep it? How can life require that of us?

YOUNG WOMAN. And yet we must.

JENNY. Must we?

A moment. Enter ISAAC, *who sees* JENNY *first.*

ISAAC. Miss Hodge, I do fear the time has come . . .

JENNY *nods to* MARY.

Mary.

JENNY. Mr – Gulliver. I must speak the prologue in your costume. As you say, the time has come.

She goes out. The YOUNG WOMAN *watches* MARY *and* ISAAC.

MARY. Isaac. How on earth . . . ?

ISAAC. I be here under the protection of the king. Till the end of the performance.

MARY. And then . . . ?

ISAAC. Then I must flee. Abroad. Do you still come with me?

MARY. Oh, Isaac . . .

ISAAC. 'Let's tear up our old lives, and make a new one.' What you said you wanted, I can give you . . .

MARY. Yes.

ISAAC. Mary, you do stay, 'tis over.

MARY. I know.

Enter LUCY.

LUCY. Oh, Mr Swift. I do come to tell Miss Stickland . . .

ISAAC *throws a desperate look to* MARY.

MARY. That the time has come.

ISAAC hurries out. Everyone involved in the opening chorus is headed to the stage. ISAAC holds back, but ANN HAZARD, at the end of the line, sees him and gulps. ISAAC puts his finger to his lips, and ANN HAZARD follows the others to the stage. JENNY is hurrying towards the stage to do the prologue. Back in the wardrobe.

Are you still there?

YOUNG WOMAN. Yes.

MARY. If so, teach me to dance.

Offstage, we hear the fanfare from the beginning of the play.
The first few lines of the Prologue cover the stage swinging
round and our mix into the end of the play.

JENNY. Good gentles, and most gentle Majesty:
  A fanfare heralds high solemnity.
  So who is this poor creature to aspire
  To act as prologue, in this mean attire?

And suddenly, all around the theatre, we see moments from
the play-within-the-play, in tableau, taking us from the
opening Prologue to . . .

Scene Eight – 'A time to keep'

In the theatre, the end of the play, watched by the ROYAL
PARTY, *a bad-tempered* EARL, *the* EXCISE MEN, *a shaken*
but stiff-upper-lipped JOHN MANFIELD, MARIA *and her*
WHIST GROUP *including* HENRIETTA, *and many other citi-*
zens; maybe even, who knows, the odd SMUGGLER *in heavy*
disguise. On stage, a Breugelesque festive carnival, with BEER-
and PIE-SELLERS, PAMPHLETEERS, SINGERS,
PREACHERS, ENTERTAINERS, PEDDLARS *and*
BEGGARS. *General ribaldry and debauchery, through which*
comes a mournful procession: we realise this represents the
Hang Fair that took place on the day of Mary Channing's
execution. MARY *as Mary Channing is led by* GEORGE *as the*
Under-Sheriff, OLD LEE *as Reverend Hutchins,* USLAU *as*
another Priest, and BRINE *and* HAGLEY *as Prison Guards.*

Booing and cheering. Through the general mêlée we become
aware of one PAMPHLETEER *selling copies of Mary Chan-*
ning's confession, and a competing PAMPHLETEER *an*
advance copy of her last words.

KIELMANREGGE *waits as the Executioner by a stake sur-rounded by faggots. Among the watchers are* EDITH *and* JOHN FEAVER *as Thomas Channing's parents and* ROBERT *and* JANE *as Mary Channing's. Also, friends we recognise from the wedding scene, played by* LUCY, MARY SUSANNAH *and various others.*

OLD LEE. To every thing there is a season, and a time to every purpose under the heaven: a time to be born, and a time to die; a time to plant, and a time to pluck up that which is planted.

GEORGE *takes* MARY*'s arm and leads her gently to the stake; she looks round at her parents and, for a moment, at Thomas' parents, and seems to be agitated, and tries to pull away; as* OLD LEE *carries on intoning.*

A time to mourn, and a time to dance; a time to cast away stones, and a time to gather stones together; a time to embrace, and a time to refrain from embracing; a time to get, and a time to lose; a time to keep, and a time to cast away.

GEORGE *repeats the court's sentence as* KIELMAN-REGGE, BRINE *and* HAGLEY *help* MARY *on to the pile of faggots. Drumming.*

GEORGE. I, as Under-Sheriff of the County of Dorsetshire, by order of the Dorchester Assize, do declare that Mary Channing is, for the crime of petty treason, namely the premeditated murder of her husband Thomas, sentenced to death by fire. Condemned prisoner, do you have anything to say before the sentence is carried out?

A moment, followed by cries of 'Get on with it!', 'Burn the fornicator!' then:

If not then, pray, proceed –

MARY. Yes, I do. I do have something to say.

Some cheers. The PAMPHLETEER *selling her last words corrects his pamphlet against delivery.*

First of all, to say before God and these people that I am guilty, even though I may have been provoked by circumstance.

Some cheers but also boos.

Then to the loved ones of my poor, dear grocer, that I was wrong to take him from you.

Some 'so I should think'-ing.

Then to . . . then to . . . my husband . . .

Some worry she might be losing her mind – 'He's dead, isn't he?', 'Is she mad?', 'Well, you'd be mad if they were going to roast you like a pig.'

GEORGE. Mrs Channing . . .

MARY. Who, if he were here, this is what I'd say.

Music as WILLIAM *appears in front of her.*

You offered me all you had, but it wasn't enough for who I had become. I'm sorry I could not . . . and never could, love you.

She looks around, sees ISAAC *as Mary's lover, maybe there, maybe in her mind.*

And to the man who told me I could ride and dance, who offered me the sands of Egypt and the wide plains of America . . . To the man who makes me want to fly . . .

MARY *is leaving the script.* GEORGE, KIELMANREGGE *and others are worried about what is happening.*

You will always make me want to stretch my wings, to fly, to dance. But now I speak in a clear voice. We cannot fly together. I cannot tear up my life so far and write a new one.

On one side of the wings, we see ELIZABETH MEECH *with the book, alarmed that* MARY *is improvising. On the other side,* JENNY *waves, gesturing that everything is all right.*

But . . . for all that . . .

Everyone looks on.

We are not parting. The things we did, the marriage of our spirit will be ours to keep for ever. Whatever burdens I must carry, whatever perils I must face. You will touch everything I do.

She looks to her family, then to ISAAC.

ELIZABETH MEECH (*prompts*). – 'Madam, unless I do this now . . . '

KIELMANREGGE (*coming in with the line, even though it isn't the right cue*). Madam, unless I do this now, I cannot protect you from the flames.

MARY (*looking at* ISAAC, *realising this will be the last time she ever sees him*). Then – yes . . . my heart is flying. But my body cannot move.

ISAAC *comes to her and looks up at her.*

ISAAC. Then – yes . . . it's time.

He reaches up and hands the fobwatch to MARY.

MARY. What's this?

ISAAC. Think how you be brought up. Think how 'tis paid for. And by whom. The time you want to keep.

MARY *looks at* ISAAC *in alarm.* HAGLEY *quickly ties* MARY's *body to the stake as* KIELMANREGGE *puts a rope round her neck and strangles her. Suddenly, music swells and effects flood the stage: dancing flames, billows of smoke, surrounding and then concealing* MARY, ISAAC *and* WILLIAM. *This builds to a huge climax, when* MARY *is revealed, hanging blackened on her stake.* WILLIAM *as the ghost of Thomas Channing stands there, but* ISAAC *has gone. Tableau. Then, as it breaks:*

FIRST EXCISE MAN (*in the audience*). Look, he's gone.

SECOND EXCISE MAN. Dammit.

FIRST EXCISE MAN. After him!

THIRD EXCISE MAN. Traitor!

MARY, having stepped down from her stake, looks on in panic. The three EXCISE MEN *stand to go as the music starts for the final song.* KING GEORGE *rises.*

KING GEORGE. Stop! You, stop, I say!

The music grinds to a halt. The EXCISE MEN *look round.*

Yes, you. Where do you think you're going?

THIRD EXCISE MAN. Um, we are about the King's business, sir.

KING GEORGE. I am the King. And my business is here. Is the play concluded?

The ACTORS *look round.* JENNY, HENRY *and* ELIZABETH MEECH *come on from the wings.*

JENNY. No, sire.

ELIZABETH MEECH. There is a song.

MARY. And . . .

HENRY. And a dance.

OLD LEE. And a reprise.

PRINCESS AUGUSTA. Oh, good.

PRINCESS MARY. Can't wait.

KING GEORGE. Then, sirs. Be seated! And let the song, dance and reprise commence!

As the EXCISE MEN *sit down, the* ACTORS *return to their places and the* MUSICIANS *prepare.*

MARIA. You know, Miss Stickland, it will be something of a relief to play a quiet hand at whist.

ELEANOR. With our tea and cakes.

FANNY. And kitty.

HENRIETTA. Every Tuesday.

*The music starts, introducing the rousing closing song of the
1804 Dorchester play. The song involves a dance, during
which* MARY FRAMPTON *and* HAGLEY *require no
encouragement to partner up, and* MARY SUSANNAH *and*
BRINE *display more than theatrical affection. Inspired by
this,* KIELMANREGGE *rushes into the audience, scoops up*
HENRIETTA, *and takes her in his arms on to the stage. Not
to be outdone,* USLAU *sweeps* ANN HAZARD *across the
floor.*

COMPANY.
    Here's a health to the farmer and God speed the plough
    Send him in his fields a good crop for to grow
    Send him in his fields a good crop for to grow
    That all things may prosper which he take in hand,
    For the farmer indeed is a capital man.

    Chorus
    Plough and sow, reap and mow
    Lambs to rear and sheep to shear
    Health and contentment to everyone here.

    Here's a health to the townsman, his work and his pride,
    And all that his knowing and skills may provide,
    And all that his knowing and skills may provide.
    Confectioners, milliners, bringers of cheer:
    Let's raise to them all a glass of fine beer.
    (*Chorus*)

    What wondrous inventions, what mighty events.
    What will life be like here two centuries hence,
    What will life be like here two centuries hence?
    Ever grander our buildings in wood and in stone,
    Ever wider our highways and brighter our homes.
    (*Chorus*)

*Then, during the last verse, the stage is flooded by friends
and relations who go up to embrace and congratulate their
loved ones.* JENNY *and* HENRY *congratulate each other.*
ELIZABETH MEECH *looks on wistfully.* NATHANIEL
approaches his daughter MARY.

Prosperity, plenty, peace, happiness, joy:
These words for our future we surely employ.
These words for our future we surely employ.
With God as our guide and his word as our stay
Our past and our future is present today.

Just as NATHANIEL *arrives at* MARY, *she holds up the fobwatch to him and waves it. She knows, and he knows she knows. Above them* ISAAC *and* MARY CHANNING (*the* YOUNG WOMAN) *are watching.*

We present you our past and our future today.
We present you our past and our future –

EARL. A *play*?

Blackout.

The End.

Afterword:

'The Community Play and the Genesis of the Social Actor'

In 1974, Ann Jellicoe, an established playwright, theatre director and Literary Manager of the Royal Court Theatre, was feeling dissatisfied with the theatre in London, and decided to leave and move to Lyme Regis in Dorset. The old instincts however had not died, so she asked the local school if they would like her to write a play for them. She set the play in Lyme Regis during the Monmouth Rebellion of 1685, and wrote on such a large scale it became necessary to involve not only the children but also the wider community. Ann brought in professional theatre friends to help with the making, but involved the energy of huge numbers of local people. It proved to be a major object lesson; the more that people were asked for help, the greater became the interest in what was happening. The greater the interest, the more people helped, and commitment grew. An amazing energy emerged; long-lost feelings of belonging to a place and a community began to surface. The play became a topic of conversation in the pubs and shops. *The Reckoning* was a promenade production, a relatively little-known style at the time; it had come about almost by chance – by a kind of serendipity. It was only in hindsight that Ann realised the measure of what had happened, and that perhaps, unwittingly, she had created a new form of theatre. It established the basic elements of what has now become known as the community play. It was especially written for and about the town, involved a professional production team and was open to anyone who wanted to participate.

Following the experience of *The Reckoning,* Ann set up the Colway Theatre Trust to develop the concept, and established what was to become a pattern and rhythm of work for the next decade. In the period between 1978 and 1985 she was responsible for producing eight West Country community plays. It became a custom that she would invite the best possible writers to her productions in order to persuade them to write for Colway. Because the work was so evidently innovative, she was able to attract writers such as Howard Barker, Charles Wood and David Edgar. David was riding a crest when Ann invited him to see her second Lyme Regis play, *The Western Women*. He had only recently finished *Nicholas Nickleby* for the RSC and the production was on its way to Broadway – he was in huge demand. One might think it was not the best of times to ask, but Ann was so convinced of the importance of the work, she believed an invitation to any writer a great opportunity for them. Writers will only take on these vast projects with such small financial rewards if they see the extraordinary potential and significance; to David's credit he not only saw it, he embraced it. David's understanding of the concept was evident in his decision that each of the 130 cast members of *Entertaining Strangers* should play a character who really existed, that they should be able to look in the local records and find out more about who they were playing. It demanded a huge amount of investigation from the local research team that gathered around him, but I am certain that the sense of responsibility, connection and ownership it engendered was the inspiration that led Dorchester to go and produce four further community plays – culminating now with *A Time to Keep*.

In the lead-up to David's first Dorchester Play, Ann had decided this would be her last as director of Colway. Her resignation followed South West Arts inexplicable decision to halve the company's tiny grant. Community plays in the south-west had become highly prized events: ironically, as the echoes of protest died away, *Entertaining Strangers* and my independent production of Nick Darke's *Ting Tang Mine* were remounted at the National Theatre, running consecutively in their 1987 season – evidence that there was a growing national respect for the work.

During the debacle, Ann asked if I would take over the reins of Colway. I joined her on *Entertaining Strangers* as co-director and to prepare for the work ahead. Since then I have gone on to direct, write or produce thirty community plays, taking the concept to Canada, America and mainland Europe. Colway and now Claque have created plays for rural villages, towns and cities. The plays have been performed in barns, schools, the ruins of a mill, churches, factories, tents, a castle, and in woods, but only once in a theatre – paradoxically, theatres rarely make the best venues. Each play project has had distinct elements and demanded different approaches, forcing me each time to reappraise exactly what a community plays was. I have found, however, that there must be certain criteria in place before I will work with a community. Foremost, the plays should be inclusive – anyone can take part. Then there has to be enough time (no less than eighteen months) to carry out a specified process for finding the play that involves a writer of quality working collaboratively with the community. I always insist there should be a local steering committee driving the project, and helping to define and implement its social agenda. The plays themselves should implicate the audience, and have high aspirations to produce real works of art. The process, properly executed, should not only support personal and social development but also set the foundations that enable the community to continue a sustained programme of cultural activities beyond the life of the play.

The work is demanding, exhausting and makes me feel very exposed. Though I often long for the sanctuary of conventional theatre, I know that community plays have more potential to be radical and subversive. Regular theatre audiences can leave a performance elated and enlightened, but in time those feelings generally fade away. Here is the community play, an art that touches people to an extent that adjusts their long-term attitudes and changes their lives; I receive letters and meet people years after their plays are over who tell me this is so. I believe this is because actors who live and work in the community to whom they perform are uniquely placed to offer something professional actors can't. I first became aware of this during the first community play I saw, Howard Barker's *Poor Man's Friend*. The experience was full of startling revelations, but one scene changed my view of theatre for ever. The scene was a courtroom. Magistrates behind high desks addressed us, the audience, as members of the court. The cast pressed round us, muttering dissent at us as if we were court attendees. A judge was delivering a sentence of death on a young boy for burning down a flax field. An eight-year-old girl in costume, standing next to me, grabbed my hand. We looked at each other. 'Why?', she asked, and I knew she demanded a response. Here was a child of today identifying with an ancestor of her community 200 years ago; pulling me in, implicating me in her world, bringing the past into the present. I can't remember what I murmured back, something like 'sorry', I expect. The point is I felt the hurt, anger and impotency to do anything that this community must have felt at the time this boy had been sentenced to death. But I wasn't just observing events, the events were happening to me. It was a profound moment that changed the direction of my life; I knew this was the theatre I wanted to be working with.

In 1990, I was invited to work in Eramosa, a rural community in Canada that was concerned about uncontrolled development on prime agricultural land around their village. The process involved the community sharing their concerns in what we have come to call 'soundings'; public meetings that try to identify and explore the most potent contemporary issues. *The Spirit of Shivaree*, written by a local writer, Dale Hamilton, expressed both the community's anger and their sense of history. Following the play, a group from the cast felt motivated to write an alternative township plan for their local council. When that failed they stood against and replaced the council, and within three years had control of the development. I believe the play had united and motivated them in three important ways: they had become informed; they had a more profound sense of history and belonging; and they had developed the confidence to feel they could make a difference.

When I returned to England, I wrote and co-directed *Vital Spark* for Hull about the women who had campaigned to improve safety conditions on trawlers after three had sunk in the storms of 1968. The real campaign women informed the younger women in the cast who were to play out their experiences. It was, in the words of one of the campaign women, '*a chance, at last to exorcise our ghosts*'. The same was true when I worked with the miners of Aylesham in 1996, where they still held onto the bitterness of the miners' strike. Here there were two camps with different agendas, one group of people wanted a play that would show their children how the village arose out of the depression of the twenties, the growth and life of the community through five decades of change; another group – albeit smaller – wanted to express their anger in a play about the strike. We decided that the first idea was a subject for their community and the second for communities outside of Aylesham. So firstly I wrote *Over and Under the Earth*, which was performed in a circus tent on the grounds of the welfare club. The second became the first touring community play, *Fightback*, which I wrote for eight community actors. Each of these community plays demonstrate that they are capable of galvanising and motivating groups of people who feel they have lost control over their lives.

I have come to call performers who act out these potent local stories to their community, 'Social Actors'. A social actor somehow has permission to implicate the audience in the drama, because this is their home territory; the actors and audience are neighbours. Audiences are implicated the moment they step through the door, and the promenade style makes this fact more potent. The performance venues used generally consist of stages around the edge of a central area, so the actors and audience share the same space. The audience find themselves surrounded by the action of the play. There are situations in the play where the audience is addressed in a way that places them in a role. It's not that shallow kind of audience participation where people are dragged on stage to be humiliated, but an invitation to the audience to get involved in the drama as people other than themselves. There are times the audience might be addressed as a jury; an angry mob; mourners or Quakers at a meeting – all in the course of one play. Essentially, the audience is not a separate society from the actors but is embraced by the cast as members of the same group. There is a sensitivity that exists between the local audience and the local cast that can infect visiting audience members, and deepen empathy. Theatre depends on empathy, but community plays present a heightened awareness that will sometimes prompt an audience to enter the world of the play physically. The fact that the actor comes from the community makes the audience's transition from spectator to involved performer almost seamless. There's a feeling of equality and intimacy when the cast and the audience come from the same community that is quite different from the one we might experience in the face of professional celebrity.

Ironically for the social actor, expectations are higher and demands more substantial than for most professionals. Social

actors need the same skills as regular actors, but must also
emphasise and develop social and improvisational skills. In a
single promenade show, social actors play a range of styles:
proscenium, thrust stage, in the round, street theatre. They will
employ skills of social behaviour: conversation, status, negotia-
tion and so on. The plays are spectacles, so there is also a huge
dependency on mime, mask, physical theatre and visual tech-
niques. Centrally too, the cast have to work as a collective, an
ensemble not only among themselves but also with the audience. We are discovering strategies to entice audiences to attend
or participate at a deeper level by stopping the play to reflect,
involving them in ritual, interjecting probes and questions; practices perhaps more associated with educational drama than
theatre. In all this I'm determined not to bully but to edge the
audiences in unawares. It's always my goal in rehearsals and
performances to use the dramatic situation to remind the group
that we can all find something of significance in everything that
has ever happened, is happening, or will happen in the future.
Theatre can help build our belief in the dramatic events, but
once that is established, the social actor can move the audience
towards a depth of insight about the experience. When that
child confronted me, theatrical convention had led me to believe
I was in a courtroom – but she took me one step further into a
moment of new awareness. True, gut-level drama has to do with
us at our deepest level, knowing what it is to be human. How
would you act under pressure? Do you change in extreme situations? What can you discover about yourself as you respond to
a threatening event? You can only make these discoveries inside
the events. These are the boundaries I want to push – where the
audience learns something about themselves because they are
placed inside situations, rather than watching other characters
respond in theirs.

The dilemma of community plays is that they are one-offs, and
the three months' rehearsal is barely enough time to teach
people to be social actors, never mind develop the concept.
There may be a downside having 'untrained' actors without the
voice or technical skills to support their performance. It's been
interesting working on *A Time to Keep*, because it's
Dorchester's fifth community play – unique in my experience.
Here are actors who know what promenade means and an

audience growing used to the style, so it's possible to open the boundaries a bit more. I am now based in Kent, and we have plans there to not only build a local tradition of plays but to create a centre where we can develop performance skills, the concept of the social actor, as well as 'seasoning' or training audiences to their role in the performance. I am sure that working with the same community again and again – building a performance centre, experimenting long term with local audiences – will develop our perspective on how to present community plays: how plays should be written, what's written, how they are staged and designed. They are still, as yet, a great untapped art form.

Jon Oram
Director, A Time to Keep
Artistic Director, Claque Theatre

Jon Oram left school, joined a circus and then trained as a drama teacher before becoming an educational drama advisor for Norfolk. He then trained as a mime, and embarked on a world tour with his one-man show. His first community play was in 1982 as assistant to Ann Jellicoe, before becoming Southwest Art's theatre animateur for Cornwall where he wrote, directed and performed for Kneehigh Theatre. In 1985 he became Artistic Director of Colway Theatre Trust, since re-branded as Claque. Jon has developed community plays extensively over that past 25 years, and has taken the work to Europe and North America. Dorchester's A Time to Keep *is his 29th community play. He is currently writing a book,* The Social Actor – Theatre Games for Groups, *and has just applied for planning permission to build a straw-bale performance centre to explore further the concept of community plays.*

Other Titles by David Edgar

ALBERT SPEER
CONTINENTAL DIVIDE
DR JEKYLL AND MR HYDE *after* Stevenson
EDGAR: SHORTS
PENTECOST
PLAYING WITH FIRE
THE PRISONER'S DILEMMA
THE SHAPE OF THE TABLE

Other Titles in this Series

AFTER MRS ROCHESTER
Polly Teale
based on the life and work of Jean Rhys

ANIMAL FARM
Ian Wooldridge
adapted from George Orwell

ANNA KARENINA
Helen Edmundson
adapted from Leo Tolstoy

ARABIAN NIGHTS
Dominic Cooke

BEAUTY AND THE BEAST
Laurence Boswell

A CHRISTMAS CAROL
Karen Louise Hebden
adapted from Charles Dickens

THE CLEARING
Helen Edmundson

CORAM BOY
Helen Edmundson
adapted from Jamila Gavin

EMMA
Martin Millar & Doon MacKichan
adapted from Jane Austen

FAUST – PARTS ONE & TWO
Howard Brenton
after Johann Wolfgang von Goethe

5/11
Edward Kemp

GONE TO EARTH
Helen Edmundson
adapted from Mary Webb

HIS DARK MATERIALS
Nicholas Wright
adapted from Philip Pullman

HOLDING FIRE
Jack Shepherd

GREAT EXPECTATIONS
Nick Ormerod & Declan Donnellan
adapted from Charles Dickens

IN EXTREMIS
Howard Brenton

JANE EYRE
Polly Teale
adapted from Charlotte Brontë

THE LIBERTINE
Stephen Jeffreys

MADAME BOVARY
Fay Weldon
adapted from Gustave Flaubert

MARY BARTON
Rona Munro
adapted from Elizabeth Gaskell

THE MILL ON THE FLOSS
Helen Edmundson
adapted from George Eliot

NORTHANGER ABBEY
Tim Luscombe
adapted from Jane Austen

PERIBANEZ
Tanya Ronder
adapted from Lope de Vega

SLEEPING BEAUTY
Rufus Norris

SUNSET SONG
Alastair Cording
adapted from Lewis Grassic Gibbon

VERNON GOD LITTLE
Tanya Ronder
adapted from DBC Pierre

WAR AND PEACE
Helen Edmundson
adapted from Leo Tolstoy

WE HAPPY FEW
Imogen Stubbs